Music as the Source of Learning

Music as the Source of
Learning

Dr. Audrey S. Wisbey

Consultant in Early Childhood and Remedial Education
and Educational Technology

University Park Press
Baltimore

In order to help develop an understanding of the needs of the normal intelligent child who is underachieving in the essential skills, reading, writing and spelling, Dr A. S. Wisbey has spent several years in forming a charitable trust entitled The Association for Children's Learning Problems.

This Association researches into the full range of causes of problems, organizes an Advisory Service for teachers and parents, trains teachers, paramedics and medical practitioners, prepares remedial programmes and organizes diagnostic and treatment clinics.

Enquiries: *16, The Plantation*
 Worthing
 Sussex

Published in USA and Canada by
University Park Press
233 East Redwood Street
Baltimore, Maryland 21202

Published in UK by
MTP Press Limited
Falcon House
Lancaster, England

ISBN 0-8391-1648-9

LCCN 80-53724

Printed in Great Britain

Contents

In memory of my parents Mary and William Douch who made it possible for me to do the work I love, and of Michael Sells of I.T.M. who encouraged and supported me.

With grateful thanks to Stanley Grundy who has latterly sponsored my research, and my husband Wally who types incessantly and 'keeps my feet on the ground'.

Introduction

The evidence grows daily that much learning failure results from undetected early childhood hearing problems (Gordon 1977).

This is because the child is deprived of the state of acute hearing sensitivity normally present at birth which makes it possible to recognize the loudness levels and duration of each individual sound. This is how a child learns the significance of the slightest variations in the quality of each sound as he collects information from the environment through all his senses, and the meaning of these changes is experienced and understood. As a result of normal sensory experience and reaction with the environment the multisensory systems are used and developed. Similarly, the growth of the brain is stimulated to make possible the storage of information and to produce the biochemical state necessary to transmit and relate the sensory information so collected and stored (Monckeberg and Prescott, 1975).

If the loudness level of sound is reduced so too is its impact. In this form a baby's normal 'startle response' to a sound, which includes the flickering open of the eyes, is rarely experienced. This response of the eyes is a seeking out of a sound source. The visual localizing of sound sources, leading to the anticipation of their spatial position, arises from the ability to hear the fine changes of pitch and loudness levels involved in movement. This in turn leads to the development of the eye movement which is so essential to literacy. It also controls both the development of hand/eye coordination (one of the basic problems involved when reversals occur) and the development of spatial awareness. A unilateral hearing loss, however slight, distorts the direction of a sound source and consequently initiates left/right confusion (Wisbey, 1979).

A further consequence of hearing loss, therefore, is failure to reach out to sound sources, so there is a reduction in kinaesthetic experiences required for motor control and coordination involved in handwriting. This is further aggravated by a lack of movement response to the changes of sound that would normally be made as a result of the continued monitoring of information to the brain through the senses.

The child with a simple hearing loss present during this early childhood stage may outgrow the problem or receive clinical treatment. But though the cause may have been removed the consequences remain untreated. Clinical tests may reveal little or no hearing defects; the widespread nature of the immaturity frequently leads to the assumption that there is brain damage, without evidence of this.

Failure to involve the child in suitable sound-making activities during this critical period of early childhood, thus making it impossible to observe his response or lack of it at

this stage is, in my opinion, the root cause of the problem. An appropriate treatment can hardly be sought if one remains unaware of a problem, so a consideration of 'suitable activities' is therefore essential. I believe them to be musical, and I shall explain why.

The young baby's hearing is at first very similar to that of the wild animal in the jungle (Elder). The softest and most strange sound causes the animal to 'freeze', while it waits to find out whether the sound means potential food or possible foe, or maybe something that can safely be ignored. The baby behaves in exactly the same way, 'freezing' momentarily, flickering his eyes open at any strange sound. This develops into his first attempts to use his eye muscles to visually fixate on a sound source. When a sound has been experienced many times, so that the baby can also observe its source and thus collect its meaning, the sound source becomes of interest, and both baby and animal begin to respond to the meaning of this sound. As this develops, the startle response (freezing) begins to fade but attempts, including visual tracking, are made to maintain interest in the sound source.

A sound that is regarded as being of no importance however loud it may be is soon ignored by both baby and animal. This is shown by the baby as early as two months of age. At the sound of his food being prepared he soon shows two responses (Bunch, 1943): he looks towards the source of the interesting sounds and begins to lick his lips. If unfamiliar utensils are used which cause a different sound to be heard, then a startle response to the new sound and curiosity as to its meaning will make the baby look in the right direction, but there will be no licking of lips. Any mother can demonstrate this when preparing her baby's food.

It is the variation in pitch, duration and intensity levels and tone that gives meaning to what is heard. A child unable to hear these differences is collecting neither meaning nor the wide range of multisensory experiences that result.

Quite loud everyday noises, to which the baby or the animal are accustomed are ignored, and yet the softest, but strange sound cause an immediate response. The apparently sleeping dog quickly lifts his ears, alerting his eyes as he waits for the origin of the sound to appear, and he is ready for instant action. The baby's reaction in similar circumstances is very much the same. It is therefore important to realize that initially, as the sound is being heard, its meaning has to be collected through the other senses, which must therefore be operating efficiently in order to play their role.

How can a child learn to recognize and associate, for instance, the barking of a dog, if the child hears only the barking but *never actually sees a dog* in the act of barking? This surely becomes a meaningless noise to be safely ignored. Consider therefore the difficulty of the visually impaired child; unless very energetic action is taken to teach him the meaning of the sounds he is hearing, through his other senses such as the tactile sense, the sounds could remain meaningless and he would have difficulty in remembering them. Remember that current hearing can only be used to recognize those sounds that previous learning has made possible. It is, of course, impossible to recognize anything not previously learnt.

On the other hand care must also be taken that a child does not become too dependent on 'seeing' and so fail to develop *listening* skills. Suitable games to make him discriminate between sounds without being able to see their source should be carried out daily.

It is as well to remember also that if any early childhood problems caused distortion of what is heard or seen, it is the distorted sound or image that was learnt. Corrected hearing or vision produce sounds and images new to the child, so the period of learning is the same as for anything else which is new.

Learning for the first time when a child is older is more difficult as the brain growth is more stabilized and with the ageing process the functioning of the sensory organs is changing.

In the case of hearing, some sounds may well have passed out of the hearing range and the memory of newly learnt sounds becomes increasingly shorter in span as the child moves towards puberty. As we become older we are increasingly more dependent on the learning of sounds that took place during the early years, when normally they could be heard in their entirety. It is vital, therefore, to ensure that this learning goes on, and to understand the consequences if it is prevented for any reason.

Each sound is a musical chord – a collection of sounds of different pitch. If we liken each sound to a lamppost, for instance, we see that those sounds that are similar and therefore most easily confused all have the same kind of post, but the lamps at the top are all different shapes and colours. When we can see the whole lamppost there is no problem in telling one from the other, but if we cannot see the lamp at the top because, say, fog obscures it, then of course they may all seem to be the same, or the colour of the lamp seeping through the fog has changed from its original colour also causing uncertainty and confusion. If we cannot rely on our memory of what is at the top, how can we then correctly identify each lamppost? If we think of our ability to hear high-pitched sounds that diminishes as we grow older, or during certain childhood conditions rather like a fog coming down, we can begin to understand why some children may have difficulty in discriminating between sounds that are very similar. Spelling too requires a very fine discrimination between sounds before correct matching to visual symbols is possible.

To take another analogy: if we look at a chair we can see its shape; we can look at it all day if we so wish, exerting no more effort than that required to keep our eyes open. While we are doing this, we also notice the uses to which the chair is being put, thus collecting information to understand the purpose of such an object. In this way learning takes place with very little effort, and the very process of learning stimulates development. With hearing, however, this is not possible because of the nature of sound; it must be made before it can exist, it cannot just 'sit in front of us' indefinitely unless an effort is made to create it, and the simultaneous collection of meaning often requires organization by another person. It is the transient and ephemeral nature of sound that makes all auditory skills dependent on memory. We cannot discriminate between pitched sounds or organize them into the sequential patterns required for language, if we can neither remember them nor hear the small changes of pitch, volume and duration involved in continuing speech. So prelanguage auditory training must involve activities centred around pitched sounds of varying volume and duration. This can only be done through music. Even if only a few of these pitched sounds are missing it interferes with the pattern. The nature of sound also means that the infant is totally dependent on a caring adult to give him the opportunity to develop this vital auditory memory during the early years, when he has the ability to hear all aspects of sound, and the brain (the receptor) is suitably absorbent and malleable to make permanent retention possible. This memory building cannot start too soon, as the hearing mechanism has been fully grown since about the sixth month of fetal life.

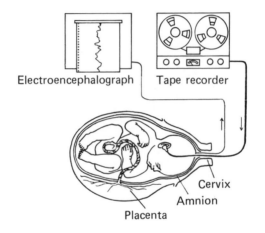

Electroencephalograph   Tape recorder

Cervix
Amnion
Placenta

Research carried out in Stockholm, Belgium, Holland, California, Japan, London and many other places is beginning to show just how much a baby learns through his hearing while still in his mother's womb. After birth, the baby can recognize recordings of his mother's heartbeats and gastric noises, sounds which are very similar to those that can be made on a low-pitched drum. As recognition requires previous learning, we must consider whether any other sounds could have been learnt during the same period. Those of us who have suffered from noisy neighbours know just how difficult it is to make any space soundproof! The baby's hearing apparatus is protected only by human tissue and fluid, so are these sufficient to provide adequate soundproofing? The use of sound under water for the detection of submarines during the last war illustrates that the fluid surrounding the baby in the womb can conduct the sound to the baby's hearing mechanism. Laboratory experiments show that human tissue, although not a particularly good conductor of sounds, does allow partial conduction (Holien and Ray).

However, all the high-pitched part of the sound would be lost, together with the finer changes in duration and loudness levels. This means that all that would remain of speech by the time it reaches the baby in the womb would be low-pitched temporal patterns. Linguists have noticed for many years that babies appear to be born with the ability to recognize such patterns (Chomsky). They claim that this proves language to be an inherent ability; but I believe that this is the result of considerable hearing experience in the womb.

Let us now consider those low-pitched patterns of sound that are available for the baby to learn in the womb. The sounds of his mother's heartbeats are supported by the feeling of vibrations. The heartbeat therefore, tends to dominate the position and absorb many of the other sounds, in effect the baby has much learning experience of simple low-pitched rhythmic patterns prior to birth, but no high-pitched sounds. From birth, however, the sound no longer has to pass through fluid and tissue, so the baby can now hear and learn the *whole* sound. At birth the sensitivity and nature of the baby's hearing make it possible to experience the exact musical pitch of individual sounds, their tonal qualities, duration and loudness levels.

Unfortunately this ability begins to fade almost from birth. The first year of life seems to be the 'critical period' for the most exact learning of sounds, with all the early years being particularly important. The biochemistry of learning would also appear to rely very heavily on both adequate and suitable nutrition *and* sensory stimulation during uterine life, and the the first five or six year after birth for the eventual achievement of potential (Monckeberg et al 1975).

Gradually learning the *meaning* of the sounds takes over from learning the exact pitch, with its variation of tonal quality, duration and loudness levels. This means that the child must rely increasingly on his memory for these aspects of *sound.* Given sufficient earlier experience, however, he can identify each sound and recall its meaning. This is not, of course, the ability to recognize and understand language. At this stage it does not matter what is said to the baby, who responds only to variations in pitch and tonal quality; an angry tone speaking the most loving words bring distress, while a loving tone using admonitory words cause an expression of joy — dogs react in a similar manner.

In other words, the normal-hearing baby has the ability to experience from birth all the sound ingredients of language, but later has to learn them to recognize, use, organize and blend them together in the form of meaningful language. Each speech sound is a complex mixture of *all* the ingredients.

If the sound ingredients of language are identified as pitch, tonal quality, duration and intensity, then one can understand the importance of learning to sing to learn these ingredients, but what has this to do with reading? Reading is basically the ability to recognize previously learnt visual symbols that represent the repertoire of speech sounds stored in the memory bank.

Obviously, then, the visual system must also be developed, but as I have explained above this is usually catered for more than adequately. However, the importance of musical activities in the child's visual development should not be overlooked. A baby may have two perfectly good eyes at birth but he has to learn to use them together in order to focus on any object. To keep objects in focus, when the person or the object or both are moving, requires an ability to make very fine and continuous adjustments of the muscles involved in eye movement. To develop this control considerable use of these muscles is essential. A baby's apparent preference for musical sounds means that the mother singing to her baby can be very important; the baby seeks out with his eyes the source of this interesting sound and so develops the ability to bring his mother's face into focus. This is probably the normal-hearing baby's first effort to focus, and greatly aids his visual development. The ability to recognize the smallest changes in pitch and intensity levels also enables the child to anticipate the spatial position of sound sources, thus making visual localizing more accurate.

As the young baby's startle response to sound also includes flickering his eyes open this quickly develops to the seeking out of the sound source. Interest is maintained by attempting to follow visually the source of the sound. The ability to hear the fine changes of pitch, tonal quality and loudness level involved in movement, distance and direction, means that the position of the source can be correctly anticipated, and visual and spatial awareness develop (Papusek, Stephens, Wisbey).

Because a baby's very sensitive hearing for high-pitched sounds makes it possible to hear the smallest changes in the quality and pitch of the sound, he will find music satisfying long before he learns to recognize the complex sound mixtures that form the content of language. Given a normal visual apparatus the binocular function so essential for literacy efficiency will develop through this.

Another startle response to sound is a movement which can be experienced through the kinaesthetic system; these sensations will, after sufficient experience, be remembered and later recalled. In this way kinaesthetic memory, motor control and coordination, and spatial awareness begin to develop and vestibular function, and the biochemistry involved, are stimulated.

The vocal exploration of a baby's speech organs that eventually, after much practice, leads to the monitored copying of speech sounds often begins as the result of a startle response to sound. Given an intact receiver and sensory system the hierarchy of learning could therefore be plotted as shown below.

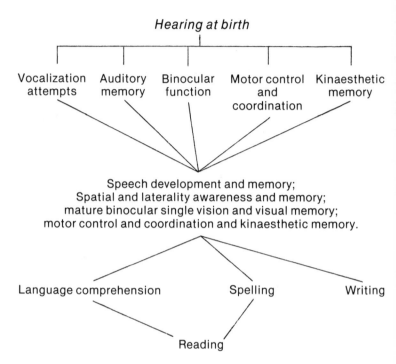

Does our teaching methodology support and, when necessary, even promote this multisensory process? If not, we will have some children failing to become literate regardless of their potential intelligence, because of some initial blockage of sensory stimulation however slight, variable and transitional. We must therefore ensure that there is no unnecessary failure; and the answer is to follow step by step the learning processes from the initial source – that is, the hearing. As the latter is musical and the necessary responses to music to be evoked are multisensory, then clearly the steps towards literacy need to be both musical *and* multisensory. (There are, in fact, five steps, and each step is dealt with in detail in the following chapters.) They must, however, be preceded by a full audiometric investigation that includes tympanometry.

When the state of current hearing has been assessed,

during which any frequently unsuspected problems in the middle ear can be discovered, then work can begin. Of course any multisensory immaturity arising from a hearing defect will also need treatment. In the case of vision there should be a full visual acuity and orthoptic check since weakness of dynamic covergence, lack of stereopsis and a failure to establish a consistent hand/eye relationship are among the many consequences of early childhood transient and minimal hearing losses. When the orthoptic assessment has been completed work on visual and spatial learning can begin.

Chapter One

The first step

What a child hears sufficiently well, often and meaningfully, is what he will learn. It follows, therefore, that if as early as possible the child can make the sound for itself without having to rely on another person, progress will be very much quicker. Looking at the way the visual system overtakes the hearing in its use for learning (Research by Socomy Vacuum Oil Co.), merely because the environment provides day-long opportunities for visual learning, shows how important it is to provide adequate opportunities to learn. Making a sound for itself also increases the learning opportunities because the child's body acts as a resonator, making it easier to hear (Sarah Munro). It has been found when teaching hearing-impaired children, that they respond to sounds at a much lower level than their audiograms would lead us to believe was possible (Wisbey, 1976), when they make the sound for themselves.

A great range of instruments is available for use but their influence on pitch learning varies considerably (Sergeant). The organ has consistently been shown to have the greatest influence on pitch learning, with the piano a close second provided the teaching method used involves evoking differential responses to each sound made (Wisbey). This variation in pitch learning according to the instrument used is possibly the result of the stable pitch sample provided by both piano and organ (we all know how important it is to have a stable learning situation). The organ also has the added advantage of being able to produce continuous stimulating tones without rapid tone decay. The increased learning possibilities provided by an instrument capable of producing continuous stimulating tones is demonstrated in Figure 1 below.

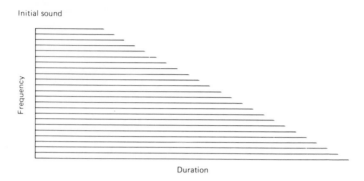

Figure 1 The analysis of a complex tone showing the gradual fading away of the higher harmonics; this is the sound generated by the striking of a piano key. Here the amplitudes of the fundamental frequency and its harmonics vary with time.

Table 1 Duration of stimulus for sensation of pitch. Demonstrates how the duration of the stimulating tone at 1000 Hz was perceived at various subjective pitches.

840 Hz when lasting 0.01   seconds
935 Hz when lasting 0.015 seconds
950 Hz when lasting 0.020 seconds
980 Hz when lasting 0.025 seconds
985 Hz when lasting 0.030 seconds
990 Hz when lasting 0.060 seconds
995 Hz when lasting 0.080 seconds
995 Hz when lasting 0.100 seconds

The decay rate of 5 dB per second in air of a tone is important, in view of the time required before experiencing the sensation of pitch. It also means that a sound heard for 8 seconds longer means 40 dB difference in hearing level. It is therefore not surprising that von Bekesy can demonstrate how pitch discrimination is better for long rather than short tones.

The works of Stevens and Ekdahl demonstrates the relationship between duration and the experiencing of the most accurate pitch sensations (Table 1).

The following graph (Figure 2) shows the duration required for a given tone to produce a definite pitch sensation. It was also found that the shorter the duration the lower the apparent pitch and, according to Ekdahl and Stevens, it is necessary for a pulse to last as long as 40 ms before the long duration pitch is established. Duration of the sound, if this affects the sensation pitch, is therefore an important factor for the teacher to consider.

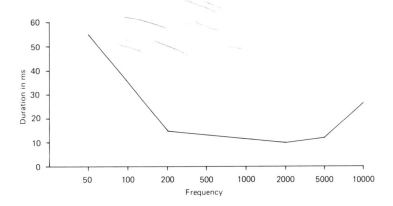

Additionally, time between each stimulus must be permitted for the buildup in response, to give the best opportunity for learning. Figure 3 shows this buildup in response evoked to a single pure tone.

Unfortunately, however, many other factors can make both the organ and the piano unsuitable and beyond the reach of the very young child for whom it is so essential to provide auditory training. One of the most important of these factors is that young children, as a result of thousands of repetitions, initially learn one pitched sound at a time (Whetnell, Fry, Love, Wisbey), and appear to be almost totally preoccupied with the exactness of each sound (Zimmerman). Given the ability to ex-

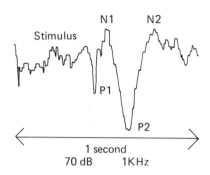

Figure 3

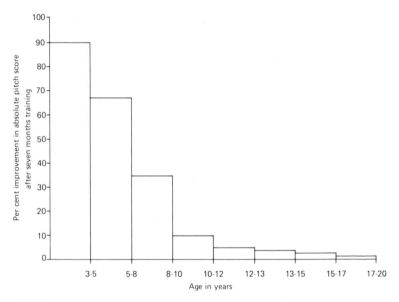

Figure 4 Ability to learn absolute pitched sounds found in the male child.

perience the finest changes in pitch and tonal quality of sounds, and the function of duration and intensity, and to collect through all his senses the meaning of such changes, the child is soon demonstrating his ability to recognize such changes. This ability however soon declines, although the rate of decline varies considerably between boys and girls (Figures 4 and 5).

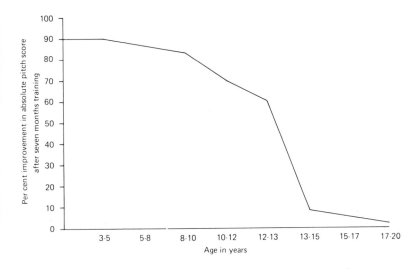

Figure 5 Absolute learning ability in the female child

As shown in Figure 5 the female child appears to remain capable of learning pitched sounds, for the first time, very much longer than the male child. It could be that the lack of suitable *early* childhood auditory experience is the reason why there are twice as many boys as girls with problems at coping with auditory memory skills, such as singing in tune and reading. Looking at the graph of the boys' ability to learn pitched sounds, it appears to match the upsurge of the male sex hormone testosterone.

I then made a study to see if there was any link with hormone levels in the girls' ability to either learn or retain pitch learning. I found the following variations during the menstrual cycle both in speed of reaction to pitch identification and in accuracy of identification (Figures 6 and 7).

I further found that the reaction time varied according to pitch, so I repeated these tests for each degree of the diatonic

27

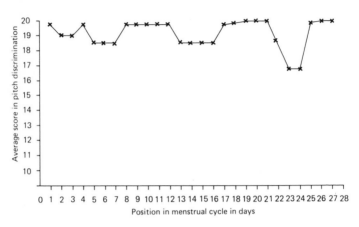

Figure 6 Pitch identification

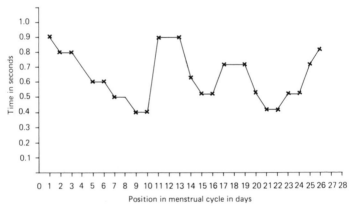

Figure 7 Reaction time (middle 'C')

scale. The following graphs (Figures 8 to 14) indicate the results obtained.

The variation of reaction time according to pitch appears to occur midcycle and is most noticeable among those degrees of the scale that took the longest time to learn, such as F, D, A, B, etc. This, plus the fact that audiograms prepared daily at the same time as the reaction tests rarely showed a matching variation of hearing levels, would suggest that it is

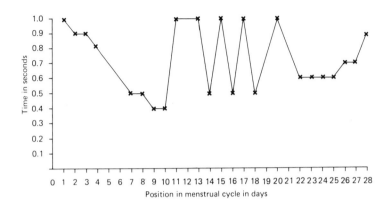

Figure 8 Reaction times for C by the same subject.

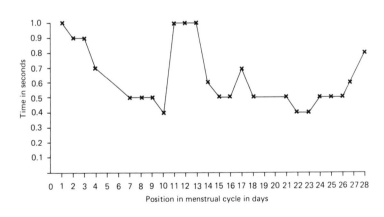

Figure 9 Reaction times for D by the same subject.

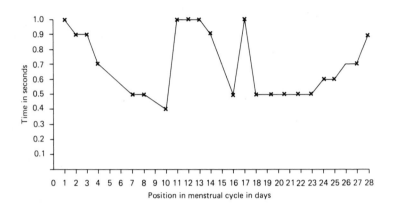

Figure 10 Reaction times for E by the same subject:

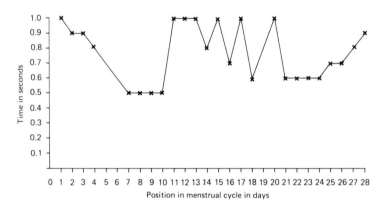

Figure 11 Reaction times for F by the same subject:

30

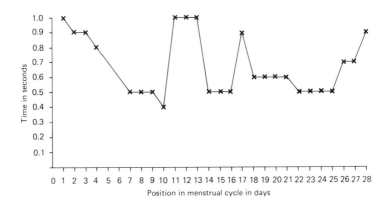

Figure 12 Reaction times for G by the same subject.

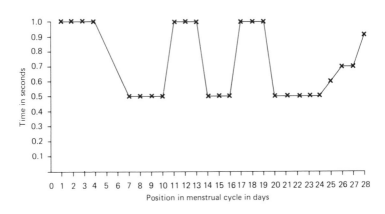

Figure 13 Reaction times for A by the same subject.

31

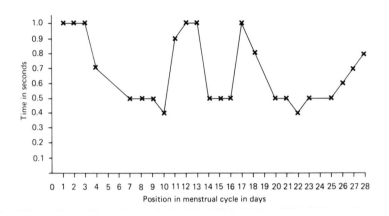

Figure 14 Reaction times for B by the same subject

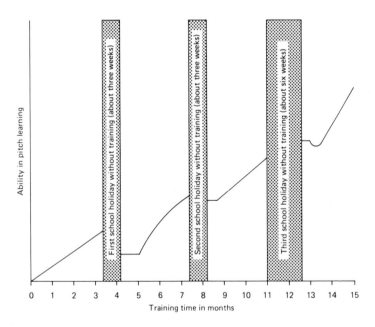

Figure 15 The time factor in pitch learning

the pitch *memory* that is affected by the hormone levels. The basic pattern in the above figures appears to match the pituitary function.

As children begin to show a decline in their ability to learn individual sounds unrelated to each other, their recognition of phrases starts to improve. Gradually at about 7 years of age this overtakes their ability to learn individually pitched sounds (Zimmerman, Wisbey, 1976).

To build up a long-term memory of each sound appears to take a period of about a year (Figure 15).

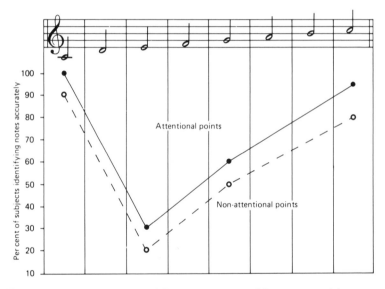

Figure 16 Attentional positions are created by notes of longer duration at phrase endings or adding stress

Dr Whetnell also found in her work at Gray's Inn Road Hospital, London that it took approximately a year's auditory training for actual listening to be achieved from the basis of the survival hearing with which we are normally born. In other words what is heard will become learnt *only* after a year's continuous experience of that hearing. This is why the child must be involved in suitable sound-making activities, evoking a variation in response, to ensure continuous learning.

The provision of a suitable instrument will give a child adequate opportunity to learn one pitched sound at a time with the minimum of dependence on another person. A glockenspiel or xylophone, with its removable tone bars and good quality sound, is a very suitable first instrument for the young child, because this type of instrument makes possible a very simple but logical, step-by-step approach. The beaters must have soft, but not woolly heads, and must make a pleasant sound that encourages learning.

The need to attract a child's attention to each individual sound is demonstrated by a research project showing how pitch learning varied according to its attentional position in material provided for learning (Figure 16).

The identification of the remaining notes appeared to depend on the accuracy of the recognition of C, E, G, C, and the learning appeared to spread to adjacent notes from these four. This test was repeated with 18-year-old teaching students who received twice weekly training. A similar pattern was shown but with the slight variation that the two Cs were identified by all, regardless of position, but with G there was still the difference according to position (Figure 17).

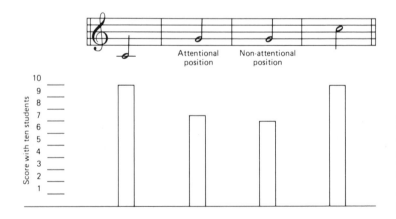

Figure 17

The test was then repeated with groups of ten preschool children, aged 3, 4, and 5 years old. They appeared to identify notes as single events unrelated to phrase position, but the pattern with these children was otherwise similar (Figure 18). If we then apply these findings to our teaching we must therefore proceed in a manner similar to the following outline.

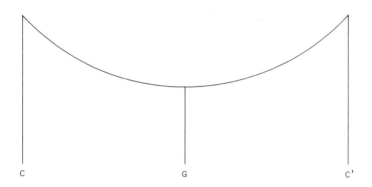

C   G   C'

Figure 18

Dr Fisch, of the Nuffield Speech and Hearing Unit in London, showed by experiment that the young child's auditory discrimination was far more sensitive early in the morning, and that auditory fatigue set in after only 10 minutes in the very young child, and brought about a delay in response. Von Bekesy found that fatigue caused apparent sharpening of pitch in the higher frequencies and flattening of pitch in the lower frequencies. An ear which has become fatigued requires a greater change of intensity before excitation and steadily becomes less sensitive to change. The prevention of fatigue and the use of the hearing at its most sensitive to enhance learning requires short training sessions early in the day. Little, early and often is therefore a very useful guideline!

Finding the first note to be learnt

Using the Xylophone, the teacher can position it so that the longest tone bar, which produces the lowest pitch sound is nearest to the player. Pick up the beater and play on each tone bar in succession, starting with the longest (lowest sound), moving up the instrument to the shortest tone bar which gives the highest sound.

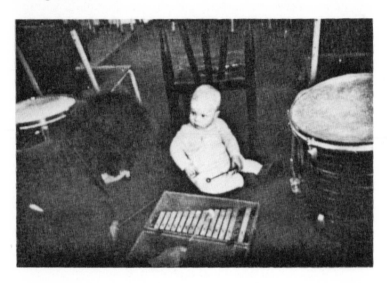

Play softly and always in the middle of each tone bar so as to produce a good quality sound (note that each tone bar has its letter name engraved on it). Sounds to be remembered must have importance and meaning for the child, and meaning must be collected through all the senses.

Activities involving the other senses provide the necessary variation and also prevent boredom. For example, to develop an understanding of 'high' or 'low', and 'up' and 'down' the use of a ladder is invaluable. Show the child what the ladder is used for by climbing up and then down the rungs, and encourage him to copy (in the interests of safety use only the first two or three rungs of the ladder). Pictures of ladders being used in the child's book also help him to develop the idea of books as a source of information.

When this is clearly understood the chlid can be taught how a 'musical ladder' is used to climb up and down the sounds, by demonstrating with the tone bar of the xylophone again from the lowest to the highest note and back again. The child can also draw a 'musical ladder' himself, drawing being a useful activity for developing hand/eye coordination. The child can play up and down the xylophone as the teacher points to each step of the ladder which has been drawn.

As the child learns one pitched sound at a time, the xylophone can then be limited to one note, by removing all the tone bars except the one marked C.

This approach supports the research findings that middle C is the first note to be learnt by the majority of children, and that for greatest efficiency of learning a note-by-note approach is required. A multiplicity of pitched sounds is frequently found to prevent the learning of any one sound (Wisbey, 1976).

The eventual increase in the span of auditory memory was also found to be related to the accuracy achieved in learning individual pitched sounds (Figure 19).

Since the ephemeral and transient nature of hearing and sound means that any auditory-based activity such as language or music involves memory, the importance of developing an auditory memory cannot be overstated. Unfortunately this is often interpreted as meaning a memory for rhythmic patterns of sound, whereas our language is made up of rhythmic patterns of pitched sounds of varying tonal qualities.

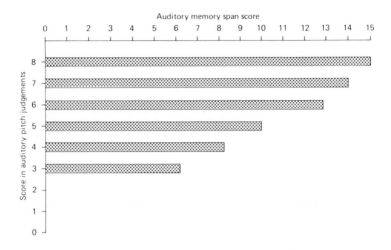

Figure 19 Auditory memory span score

As A. N. Leontiv stresses 'if conditions of an individual's life do not *require* him to distinguish sound complexes according to their basic frequencies he may not develop the capacity to do so'.

The vocalizing of sounds improves the efficiency of pitch learning. Kohler found that whenever the use of vocalization was included in pitch training the threshold of discrimination improved. Bentley found that pitch discrimination at the extreme edge of the vocal range showed two-and-a-half times more errors than in the middle of the vocal range. Franklin and Vernon found that the more limited the vocal range, the more limited the concept of tonality, with accuracy of judgement doubling when notes fell within the vocal range. Many workers have shown that the child's development of pitch memory has advanced side by side with the expansion of vocal activities.

In an attempt to assess the ability to sing in tune records were prepared of boys' progress over a period of 10 years. The results were expressed in grades of A, B, C and D and shows how the gradual drop in pitch range of hearing begins to affect the finest degree of intonation (Figure 20).

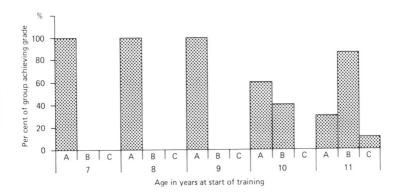

Figure 20 Results expressed in grades A, B, C and D:
A: sight-sing fluently in any key with good concentration and no mistakes;
B: sight-sing reasonably well, with occasional lapses of intonation;
C: sight-singing in tune only possible when singing with others;
D: unable to sing in tune.

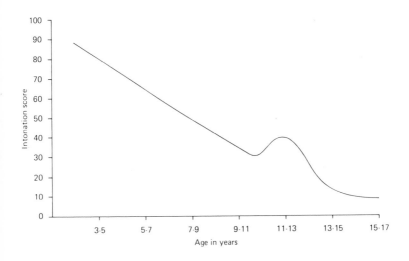

Figure 21

One other interesting factor demonstrated was the shortlived upsurge in hearing acuity and intonation that consistently appeared for a few months prior to the more obvious signs of the onset of puberty in the male child, before dropping to a fairly static standard as before (Figure 21).

Activities for practising note C

Humming is a suitable vocal activity for young children as a good quality of sound is produced without strain. I usually introduce humming by explaining to the child that all musicians tune their instruments every time they practise. Tuning in this case means playing on the xylophone in the middle of the tone bar very softly simultaneously humming the same sound — it is the sound a child makes and so hears that he eventually learns. A great deal of careful listening is essential to acquire this learning — hundreds of repetitions of the new sound are necessary, and vocalizing these sounds enhances their learning. Humming discourages shouting and encourages a pleasant quality of sound; many children can hum in tune before they can sing. This matching of the voice to an instrumental sound is the beginning of listening. The baby 'practises' vocalizing individual pitched sounds for several months, day in and day out, before it can produce at will the sound it wants. We call this practice 'babbling'.

To provide repetition of the note C games must be invented to make it enjoyable and fun for the child otherwise he will become bored and learning will cease; this is particularly evident in the case of the intelligent child who becomes bored very quickly. The sound can be played first and then hummed very softly, with the child copying this. When the humming session is over the child can close his eyes while the teacher plays a simple pattern of sounds all on the note of C — the rhythm of several well-known tunes perhaps. The patterns should not be too long; five or six sounds are as much as most children can manage, some not even that at first. The child can copy the patterns, and gradually, by means of a variety of activities, the memory span of pitched sounds can be increased.

This can be followed by a 'question and answer' game in which a short pattern of sounds is played (the question), and the child answers it by making up a pattern of sounds, all on the note C. This all helps to build up the child's span of auditory memory, an essential requirement for language.

There must be considerable listening before a sound is learnt, but do not try to explain listening to a child. Instead play games that solicit a response to the sound. This gradually teaches him the meaning of listening. (Assume he has no knowledge and teach him step by step.)

Action games are useful for this, and help develop meaning, motor control and kinaesthetic memory. For instance, the teacher plays the *sound* of an action such as walking, running or hopping and then mimes the action. The child copies the action, humming the sounds, while the teacher continues playing the sound of the action. Some suggested actions to be copied are jumping with both feet together, walking, running, marching, hopping, and perhaps skipping. Some children need considerable practice of the first four before they can manage to skip, as this action involves a kinaesthetic memory of component movements.

c

When the child can match his movements to the sounds he can then play the sounds, the teacher doing the same. These simple activities can be used to increase the child's meaningful vocabulary. When he can act and hum at the same time he can then sing the words on the note of C in small rhythmic patterns. Suitable words can be made up to match activities such as:

Crawling along the floor
Jumping with both feet
Walking along the road
Soldiers marching along
Running, running to school
Hopping on one foot and then on the other
Hopping with the left foot
Hopping with the right foot
Forwards and backwards, on the spot.

Activities to develop hand/eye coordination

While these activities provide the much-needed repetition of the sounds to be learnt, they also assist the development of motor control stimulating labyrinthine activity; they require the child to use his eyes, as any change of the child's spatial position stimulates eye movement, because he must exercise various eye muscles in order to direct the visual axis of each eye to the same object. It is only by constantly adjusting the contraction and relaxation of the individual ocular muscles, which move the eyes, that they can both retain their correct relative positions. Achieving this is important because binocular single vision is only acquired by the most perfect form of coordination between the two eyes at all times, so that the two images of a single object, formed separately in the central part of the retina (fovea) of each eye and then transmitted to the brain, are perceived there as one single image. There is much evidence to show that the functions involved in achieving the finest degree of binocular single vision are learnt during the first few years of life, and that delays in experiencing this functioning can irreparably affect the nature and quality of visual efficiency.

Normal binocular vision demands both an adequate power of accommodation (focusing) and convergence, so that when an object approaches the eyes, or vice versa, the image remains clearly fixed on each fovea without any deviation. If this fusion is not sufficiently exercised in early childhood, with the obvious results of better vision, then the desire for and the ability to achieve this perfect coordination may not develop. It must be appreciated that this is not an *inborn* characteristic, but is acquired gradually in the first few years of life, as the result of experience, and in the same way as coordinated use of the arms and legs gradually develops (Lyle and Wybar, 1977). In this way the extrinsic ocular muscles provide sensory information to the brain and also help to establish the feedback system involved in both spatial and body awareness.

Inadequate experience during early childhood, which slows down the achievement of mature development, could thus have learning consequences continuing long after maturity has been reached. These could include confusion of visual directional attack, difficulty in maintaining fine control over eye movement and a failure to establish hand/eye and occasionally hand/foot *stable* relationships. We tend to forget that skills are acquired after a massive amount of repetition of experience gained through *maturely functioning systems.* Immaturity of convergence and accommodation can also cause clumsiness as object outlines would be less clear.

Movement to music, therefore, stimulates the use of the eyes, and encourages careful listening as it requires change of movement to match changes in sound and develop greater motor control and coordination. The child's imagination can also be stimulated with suitable variation in the choice of the music and a few suggestions as to the scope of movement. In my opinion, imagination is the outcome of previous experience assisted by a little prompting in the varying of each activity. An inability to respond to the changes in music by change of movement, or uncoordination and clumsiness, can be detected and medical advice sought – maybe all that is needed is extra experience. This must, however, be investigated, as delays in sitting, crawling and walking have often been recorded in children who later have reading difficulties. Adequate experience of coordinated movement is needed to eventually make correct judgements of space and orientation.

Each activity requires preparation by both the adult concerned and the child — remember that it is often in the preparation for an activity that meaning and understanding is acquired. The adult should adopt the role of a leader guiding the child throught the activities and preparation — supporting him, providing a helping hand and advice when necessary, but not doing all the work. A visit to the zoo, for instance, where there are many birds and animals to be seen and heard, is a good starting point for such a game or activity. The greater the variety means a far wider range of tonal qualities to be heard. A small tape recorder, on a visit to the zoo to record animal sounds, can be used very successfully to help the child develop an auditory memory *if the child is present when the recording is initially made and so understands the source of the sounds*. Meaningless sounds are very difficult to remember.

Getting storybooks based on subjects such as the zoo or other places visited, from the local or school libraries, develops the idea of the book being an exciting source of information long before formal reading begins. In this way attitudes are being formed from a very early age. Recordings of bird and animal sounds and music which reproduces aspects of these sounds, such as Saint-Saëns' *The Carnival of Animals* and sound effect recordings all produce useful material for the learning of pitched sounds.

Storytime can be a very useful revision period for learning animal names and sounds, with the recordings helping to illustrate many of the stories, and at the same time giving valuable information as to the child's ability to hear the differences in sounds.

Making model animals using modelling clay, plasticine and coloured dough is another very useful activity to develop both hand and eye coordination and visual convergence sufficiency. The convergence reflex, which is part of the near reflex, is concerned with the simultaneous movement of the two eyes so that they are able to be directed to objects at varying distances from the eyes. Literacy skills are near skills, so insufficiency of convergence experience can cause problems since the position of the eyes at rest is relatively divergent.

Convergent reflexes can be initiated in several ways, such as exercising accommodation as a result of the convergence/accommodation relationship, making a voluntary effort and in response to the seeking out of a non-visual source of stimuli, such as touch, smell and sound.

Games associating sounds with information provided by the other senses should also be played, so that meaning can be collected and stored for later use. A blindfolded child listening to the sounds of cutting different objects such as a carrot, apple, bread and an onion, can be asked which one is being cut; he can then taste each object to help its identification. He must of course, first see, taste and smell the objects before he can be expected to recognize them.

Try also pouring different liquids into a jug for the child to listen to while he watches, then repeat the activity with him blindfolded. Various kitchen sounds can be identified, aided by smell and taste.

The tactile sense should not be omitted from these games. In order to hear efficiently, it is important to realize that we are normally collecting information about sounds continuously through our other senses. Touching, feeling and walking on different surfaces, listening to footsteps on wooden stairs, pavements, carpeted floors and lino, all provide added practice in distinguishing between sound qualities. A great variety of games can be improvised to further develop this ability. A blindfolded expedition around the school or classroom, for instance, can be fun and helps to demonstrate how much information is collected through hearing, whether it is the presence of objects in the way, the hearing of an echo or the nature of a room's furnishings.

The difficulties experienced by children who are born with limb or muscle deficiencies, or with quite minor hearing disorders of the type that reduces interesting variations in quality of sounds heard in the development of the finest degree of binocular function, emphasize the importance of this type of experience. Poor muscle tone can be particularly damaging to the learning of language skills, as confusion would arise from the changes in sensory experience provided by varying states of muscular efficiency caused by this lack of tone. Modelling, of the type described above, encourages the maintenance of convergence. Many activities can be provided through the medium of play to stimulate the use of the eyes at various spatial positions, and so promote the fine muscle coordination needed.

As the range of vision can be increased by the movement of the head and body, the child with binocular function problems often adopts abnormal postures in order to see better, such as turning his head to one side to aid his performance in any activity. These children can be identified by careful observation during suitable play activities, and referred for treatment.

It cannot be overemphasized that early identification and treatment is an essential priority if the child is to achieve normal binocular single vision.

Another activity to assist pitch and tonal discrimination

could be described as an animal choir practice, using a variety of toy animals to develop tonal discrimination. The choir practice must begin with tuning, the child humming the sound that each animal makes, at the same time playing on the C tone bar of the xylophone. Every animal in the choir tunes its voice, so for example, when a cat sits on a step ladder, the child becomes a cat by humming and then gradually changing the sound to 'me-ow', still on the note of C.

When a cow sits on the ladder, the child becomes a cow and tunes his voice by humming and then gradually changing to 'moo'.

When a bee sits on the ladder, the child becomes a bee.

The greater the variety of animals used in the choir practice, the more practice there is in the sound of C, and the more kinds of animals are being learnt. The child is also learning that whatever sits on the C step of the ladder must also sing that sound. This could be called the beginning of music literacy.

The study of the animals sounds should also always include their movements. The child can move like the animal as he makes its sound, and he can later play on the xylophone the rhythm of the movement that the animal makes.

Movement to music greatly increases coordination and motor control because it provides an external source of control. The discipline required for movement control can therefore be developed in a 'fun' setting by the use of suitable music which gradually requires greater control. Make sure that the movements made reinforce the understanding, by using for instance, slow-moving music to develop an awareness of slowness, and loud music with a crashing of instruments, requiring big heavy movements, to illustrate loudness. The child's movement response to music further indicates that he can *hear* the changing qualities of sound.

Any such session should be brought to an end while it is still 'fun', so that one can return to this 'fun' at the next session. Remember also that the more sessions held on the material of each stage the greater the eventual learning. So much learning failure arises from insufficient repetition, and lack of establishment of the earlier learning experiences. The more the child collects 'fun' experiences, the more material will be available later for teaching purposes. If the activities are always 'fun' no stress or anxiety will develop; this is important since stress alone can inhibit reflexes and lead to lack of coordination. As mentioned above a small tape recorder taken on an excursion can be used to collect sound effects for use when telling the child stories or when talking about previous expeditions; this both develops the child's memory and increases his vocabulary. The child can be encouraged to make up stories using these sound effects; the teacher can write down the stories as they are told, making sure the child is watching, as motivation to read and write will develop out of this part of the 'fun' activities.

Further activities aimed at increasing muscle tone and strength, increasing oxygen intake and so creating a feeling of wellbeing, developing body and spatial awareness, stimulating the use of the eyes and vestibular function should be continually used. At first, they should be practised without music, but when they are being performed accurately then matching them to music brings in an element of control and encourages the repetition needed to establish kineasethetic memory, this must be developed since literacy involves very fine control and the immmediacy of response arising from a well-established memory; an inadequate memory interrupts

49

the performance of any skill and is particularly at risk in times of stress, tiredness or ill-health.

The visual field is restricted to the extreme limits of the movements of both eyes in all directions without movement of the head or body. A lack of eye movement could be masked by compensating head and body movements; careful observation should detect this. When performing any movements the child should be encouraged to use his eyes to the maximum (exploring his limb extremities, for example).

Developing spatial and body awareness

The following activities are suitable.

(1) Curl up on the floor, and then stretch out in a 'star' shape.

(2) Standing on tiptoe, stretch up with the hands as high as possible.

(3) Stand on one leg and stretch the other leg behind as far as possible, then in front, then to the left, then to the right, saying simultaneously 'stretch to the back', 'stretch to the front', etc. Repeat with the other leg.

(4) Lie on the floor stretching out with the hands and feet, then sit up, reach out and touch the toes with the hands.

(5) Squat on the heels and then stretch up with the arms and hands.

The following activities help stimulate the good vestibular function needed for balancing skills and aid the development of spatial awareness and conjugate horizontal eye movement.

(1) Stand up and slowly rotate, alternately rolling the head with the eyes following the movement in each case.

(2) Turn head-over-heels, somersaults, handstands, cartwheels.

(3) Dance skipping round and round in circles.

(4) Hoola hoop, using PE hoops.

(5) Dance with rhumba movements.

(6) Crawl along the floor to slow music like a heavy animal; describing the animals during the actions.

The local library can probably provide a source of suitable recordings for these activities. It must be remembered that thousands of repetitions, over a period of over a year, are necessary to establish a long-term memory.

Improving muscle tone and further work on spatial learning

The following exercises are taken from the world of ballet. For these activities the use of a ballet teacher's music book would be most helpful.

(1) Holding a bar or the back of chair for support, swing one leg backwards and forwards as high as possible.

(2) Swing one leg forward and up, rise up on the toes of the supporting leg; hold this position and then push the raised leg away from the body; change legs and repeat the action.

(3) Lying on the back, sweep first one leg in a large circle and then the other.

(4) Run slowly, quickly, turning, stopping, lifting legs high, knees high, pointing toes, kick or jump in different directions, hop first on one leg and then the other; these all improve muscle tone, spatial learning, stimulate the biochemistry involved in learning and develop kinaesthetic memory.

When these simple activities can be performed satisfactorily, elementary ballet exercises can assist further development and at the same time provide a variety of activities in between the sessions of listening training.

Suggested ballet exercises

The illustrations below show a series of suggested and recommended ballet exercises.

1.   2.   3.   4.   5.

6.   7.   8.   9.

Building up movement sequences, gradually increasing in length, is yet another important factor in the activity programme for the development of memory span, for example two jumps, four walking steps, two hops on the left foot, one turn, two hops on the right foot.

A trampoline is also an excellent apparatus for use in this type of work as learning is enhanced by experiencing the accompanying vibrations.

Normal ballet training of course provides the same kind of experiences, and is an activity educationally justifiable in its own right.

All the games and activities in which movements are involved and which are of interest to the child can be explored to develop motivation and help acquire the necessary control and coordination.

An uncoordinated child would probably be considerably helped by tap dancing, particularly as the sounds of the metal plates applied to the heels and toes of the shoes attract great attention to the movement components.

Chapter Two

The Second Step

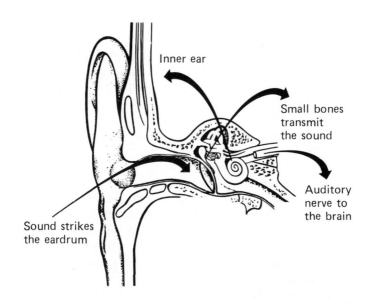

Inner ear

Small bones
transmit
the sound

Auditory
nerve to
the brain

Sound strikes
the eardrum

The physiology of sound

Sound strikes the hearing mechanism and is then transmitted
via the little bones causing them to vibrate, and pass the sound
to the auditory nerve and thence to the brain. Loudness levels
are thus learnt, but it must be remembered that the ear is not so
sensitive to small changes of loudness as it is to pitch. The
ability to recognize very small changes in loudness levels gives
the child much information about his spatial position, his

relationship to other objects and people, and the development of language, which is made up of pitched sounds of varying tonal quality in a variety of stress patterns.

Sound strikes the nearest ear first and is then directed around the skull to the furthest ear. Normally therefore, the sound is heard more loudly in the nearest ear, and as a result the brain gradually recognizes from which direction the sound source is approaching.

The child looks in that direction, monitors the approach of moving objects through his visual system, exercising his eye muscles as well as gaining spatial information, and gradually learns that the object is approaching from his left or right. If however, he has a slight hearing loss in the ear nearest to the sound source the other ear may actually process the sound at a louder level, giving the impression of the sound travelling from the *opposite* direction. If the hearing loss is variable, imagine the confusion caused when trying to learn left from right or any spatial position.

The question may be asked: 'Do such children learn to anticipate the spatial position of moving sound sources?' Difficulty in localizing such a sound source could mean that the child tends to ignore the impulse to seek out the sound source. In this way both exercising the system required for stable and mature binocular functioning, and the feedback of spatial information during exercising, is reduced. It should not be forgotten that the establishment of a mature visual system requires the same amount of experience as that of any other feedback system. In this case it is the visual sensation arising from the gradually developing ocular muscle coordination that provides the monitoring and learning processes. Any lag in the development of such coordination still provides a visual sensation *which is learnt,* and if it occurs during the initial childhood years of great neural plasticity it could well become firmly established. But if there is confusion as a result of the variable sensations arising from an unstable and immature system, then the feedback system, which requires a stable learning situation will not be established. Such maturation lags are so often stupidly ignored or dismissed with the remark

'He will grow out of it'. So we do of any problems – eventually!

Research shows that the sounds in attentional or emphasized positions in a phrase stand a much greater chance of being learnt. It is also true that the very sensation of pitch can be varied according to its loudness level (Figure 22).

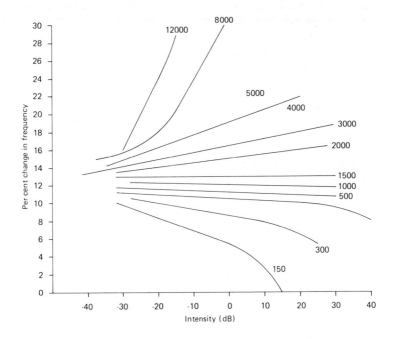

Figure 22 Contours showing how pitch changes with intensity (from Stevens 1935).

Once having experienced the full range of hearing, an awareness of aural harmonics is developed. It is the awareness of the order, duration, strength and frequency of these harmonics that leads to the identification of complex tones.

If a sound is played loudly the order of harmonics is altered, causing distortion; it is therefore important to encourage listening to each pitched sound at the softest level possible for it to heard by the individual child. In this rather noisy world of ours it is often necessary for the child's attention to be attracted again to small changes of loud and soft. This can be done through suitable games in which it is essential to use pitched sounds. It is of course, the variations in loudness levels of pitched sounds that form the basis of our language. As explained above, all aspects of sound must be experienced in a way that is meaningful to the young child, providing for the massive amount of repetition necessary for first-time learning, yet at the same time remaining 'fun',

Using model animals in tonal activities

Models, pictures of animals and toys can all be used, as in the activities suggested in Chapter 1. (The involvement of an old, precious toy in learning often produces far better results than the use of new toys bought specially for the occasion). A toy or model elephant and a tiny model of a mouse form the basis of a game to develop an understanding of the loud and soft loudness levels (at the same time providing a means of checking that the child can acutally hear the differences in the loudness levels). Homemade models made out of clay or dough are preferable as they can involve hand/eye activities.

In this game, the model elephant is placed on the ladder, and the teacher plays on the C tone bar of the xylophone very loudly, explaining to the child that the elephant makes a very loud sound when he sings.

Then the mouse is placed on the ladder while the teacher plays very softly on the C tone bar, explaining that the mouse sings with a very soft voice.

Following plenty of experience with toys and models the child can be encouraged, as a step towards symbolic representation, by drawing the three dimensional toy in single dimension form. To miss the initial experience with objects is, I believe, a grave mistake as these initiate and support stereopsis, a far higher standard of binocular function. In appreciating stereopsis one has only to look at the problems of the limb-deficient children to realize this. Once the child appreciates

stereopsis sufficiently to establish learning, he can then represent this with a single-plane drawing, while remaining aware
of its difference. If this is attempted too early, the differences
will not be recognized, and in fact the ability to develop this

awareness might be suppressed; the three-dimensional
aspect should be emphasized to continually encourage
stereoptic vision, simultaneously introducing an element of
visual control. Unfortunately, the tendency for educationalists
to become obsessed with the need to develop imagination and
creativity has frequently led to a total lack of consideration of
the physiological processes involved in learning. Consequently, children have been deprived of the opportunity to gradually
and progressively acquire the muscular control needed for all
skills. If imagination develops from varying the use of what
has been previously learnt, then it is not surprising that there
are problems in this aspect of education as well.

Visual control requires coordinated use of twelve muscles, six of each being positioned in each eye. Free drawing does not require such control, as this is the result of pulling the eyes together to fixate on a very small area. A first step towards maintaining this control is therefore performing such activities as filling or colouring in outlined shapes. Outlining the ladder and the elephant and mouse used in the above games would be of help. Joining dotted shapes also aid control, so the animals and ladder could be prepared in dotted form, for the child to complete by joining up the dots and then colouring in.

These artistic attempts, using first the elephant and then the mouse, can be followed by asking the child to reproduce on the xylophone the sounds made by each animal – playing very loudly for the sound of the elephant, and very softly for the mouse.

The next part of the game is the tuning session, which of course, begins with the teacher playing in the middle of the tone bar very softly, listening very carefully and then humming on the same sound. The child copies this, making sure that both the mouse and elephant can do the same. Other model animals can then be introduced to provide variations in loudness levels, for instance a dog sitting on the ladder, tuning his loud voice by humming before he sings 'woof-woof'. A cat could be sitting on the ladder next, tuning his voice before singing 'me-ow, me-ow'. The greater the number of animals used the more variation in tonal quality will be introduced.

A puppy could also be used to introduce a moderately loud sound, or a kitten a moderately soft sound. Acting the movements of these animals to music continues to promote motor control while reinforcing the understanding of loudness levels, provided that the appropriate movements are made. The availability of different experiences for each difference in loudness level, however small the difference limen, aid this learning. Drawing the pictures of the toy sitting on the ladder and then playing the sound, as previously explained, is a simple means of developing an understanding of the symbolic representation of sound. It also provides repetition of pitched sounds of varying loudness levels that are so necessary for learning. Some children need a great deal of practice before learning this, particularly if they suffered a hearing problem during the first year of life. Do not forget that the louder the sound must be, before it is heard at all, the greater the reduction in the variation of sounds will be experienced.

As mentioned above use of a tape recorder on expeditions to record loud and soft environmental sounds encourages the child to discuss the differences in the loudness levels.

When the child can produce the correct sound to match each animal picture, this can be followed by introducing the shorthand signs used by adults. The elephant shorthand sign is 'ff', the mouse 'pp' and the fog 'f'. The moderately loud sound of the puppy is 'mf' and the moderately soft sound of the kitten is 'mp'. I have tried this successfully with children aged 4 years but if there appears to be any confusion the teacher should carry on with the picture and sound combination, returning to the sound and sign combination later on. It is learning the sounds and providing the child with a means of identification of each variation in sound that is so important at this stage. Sounds can only be identified while they are being experienced, or remembered, whereas the sign can gradually be used to represent the picture of an object. A suitable game to help this learning is a version of the card game 'snap'. When the card picture of an elephant is played at the same time as the shorthand sign of 'ff' then *'snap'* is the answer.

Another game can be played in two ways. The teacher plays the sound and then asks the child to find the correct picture or sign, – alternatively the child looks at the picture or sign and plays the sound it represents. Plenty of time, however, should be spent on the activities where the child listens to the sound and then identifies the picture or sign – at this stage the priority is to provide sufficient listening experience. Most children have learnt to use their eyes more than their ears, so their hearing tends to become lazy. When a sound and its meaning have been learnt, ensure that the child has to use his hearing to identify the learnt sound without relying too much on help from the eyes. This can best be done by the first part of the above game where the sound is produced before the visual symbol. Various games where the eyes are blindfolded also encourage listening – the child can close his eyes and repeat the sounds or words the teacher makes or says.

The idea of doing practice or 'homework' every day can now be introduced. At this age the child thinks of such activities as being delightfully 'grown-up'. The child should be encouraged to play softly on the xylophone, and tune his voice by humming to the sound of C. A minute or so at various times of the day will provide all the practice needed. Ask the child each day if he has done his 'practice' or 'homework', making it sufficiently important to include in the day's programme of essential activities; the teacher must also practice, still keeping the activity 'fun'. A child learns what is considered to be important by observing the involvement of the adults around him. Music is not an isolated, activity but one of cheerful anticipation and participation with others.

On the piano show the child which is middle C by looking at the photograph above and then finding the correct note on the piano. The teacher can also tune the voice to the note C on the piano, but the child should not be allowed to practise on his own until he is clearly able to find the correct note without any difficulty, although he should be helped to reach this stage as soon as possible.

Progress in pitch learning according to instrumental experience is demonstrated by Figure 23 below, prepared in an experiment measuring children's progress through a training programme (Wisbey, 1976).

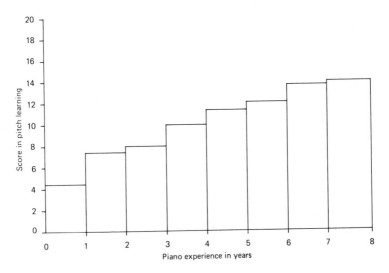

Figure 23

Games requiring the child to listen for very soft sounds unaided by his eyes should also be played. A simple game is to have the child close his eyes; the voice is tuned to the sound of C, and the teacher moves around the room playing the sounds of C very softly. The child must point in the correct direction of the sound, if he appears to have difficulty in deciding which is the direction of the sound it may be that he just needs to learn the difference in the sound levels involved. On the other hand, if the correct direction of the sound has not been learnt this may be the result of a hearing loss in one ear.

Recognizing the small changes in pitch and loudness levels that identify the direction from which a sound is coming is one of the ways in which a child develops an awareness of left and right. Games of this nature therefore have an important and additional role to play be developing the awareness of the child's spatial position while contributing to the amount of repetition of the sound needed. Many games can be improvised to help the child realize that as the sound source moves towards him, or moves towards the sound source, it appears to be louder.

Games for identifying sound sources.

The train game

A visit to the local railway station to watch and hear the trains coming in and out of the station is a very useful activity, as looking for the sound source also involves the use of the eyes.

This can be followed by looking at pictures of trains coming and going. Taking the tape recorder to the station is also very important, particularly as the child can hold the microphone or be otherwise involved in the actual process of recording.

In the classroom, playing the sounds of the trains on the tape recorder can be used to start off the train game, while both teacher and child move around the room in time to the sound, perhaps even chanting the words softly, 'clickety-clack, clickety-clack, (a very good tongue-training exercise). Louder sounds are used as the train comes nearer and softer sounds as the train moves away. The next stage is to play the train sounds of 'clickety-clack, clickety-clack' on the C tone bar of the xylophone and to hum or sing the words in tune with the note C.

In the interests of speech training the sounds of 'sh, sh' could also be added. The sounds involved in the train game are of course also working on the ability to build up sequential learning.

Next the teacher can copy the sounds of the train coming

from the distance by starting very softly, gradually getting louder and louder as the train gets nearer and nearer until it is very loud, then softer and softer until it can no longer be heard as the train disappears into the distance. Pictures can be shown to illustrate this. The child can now copy these train sounds, first by running around the room making them, and then by playing exactly the same sounds on the xylophone. The game can be varied to ensure careful listening by making the train stop occasionally at a station before moving off again; the activity stops whenever the teacher stops playing the train sounds on the xylophone.

Encourage the child also to listen for cars coming from the distance. Watching cars come and go can be a useful exercise in learning to judge distance, direction and spatial position through hearing and vision. If the child is a little clumsy it could be that he has lacked sufficient opportunity to learn this spatial position.

When the child has played the train game many times so that he can recognize and copy quite small changes in loudness levels, again show him the pictures of the train coming from the distance and then going off again, and ask him to play the sound that matches the picture. When this is easily performed it is a simple step to the use of the 'shorthand' signs.

Hunt the sweet

This game is always popular, but it needs a plentiful supply of sweets, because once the sweet is found by the child he naturally wants to eat it.

The child closes his eyes while a sweet is hidden somewhere in the room; the child then opens his eyes and starts to look for it. The teacher and the other children play on the C tone bars of their xylophones. As the child moves nearer to the place where the sweet is hidden, the playing becomes louder, and as he moves farther away from the hiding place the playing becomes softer.

The larger the group of children playing this game the

more fun it is – all children love to have the chance to find a sweet. This game also encourages considerable repetition of the sound that is being tolerated, enjoyed and in the end finally rewarded.

Activities for coordination and eye movement

Once again with ballet movements. These provide very suitable material for more complicated movements to extend coordination, and exercise the eyes.

(1) (a) Lying on the floor and on the side, push arms and legs gently backwards.

(b) As above, push back and relax.

(2) Moving freely, jump into the air, and push arms and legs backwards.

(3) (a) Sitting on the floor, legs apart, bend down first to one leg and then to the other; use arms together, one arm at a time, nose leading, ear leading. Sweep round in a circle over both legs.

(b) Arms high above the head, bend down to one leg, hold position push down a little farther and relax.

(4) Describe a circle with the hand in the air on a vertical or horizontal plane.

(5) Describe a circle as in the previous exercise, but use the shoulder, elbow or head to lead.

(6) (a) Shake the arms, hands, shoulders.

(b) Stop shaking. Stretch or reach; relax.

The vocabulary should be practised throughout each of the exercises.

Chapter Three

The Third Step

As mentioned before, the duration of a sound influences the pitch sensation arriving at the brain. Since our language is make up of pitched sounds that vary both in tonal quality and duration, it is very important to ensure that a young child can hear the differences in duration and is given the opportunity to hear them sufficiently often. When experimenting with a training programme I found that when complex rhythmic work was introduced too early it retarded pitch learning; similar findings were reported by Steiner and Teplov. I believe this to be mainly a question of duration of stimulus because of the need for this to continue long enough for the experience of pitch sensation. To further learn these differences a simple form of notation can be introduced, which will at the same time develop the idea of visually codifying the differences in sound, a process fundamental to the skill of reading.

Marilyn Pflederer-Zimmerman found that the presence of a visual cue made a significant difference in the learning of pitched sounds. A study of the work of Apel, Hyatt, Parrish, and Wolf, followed by experiments in several schools, showed that any notation providing a visual cue assisted pitch learning, if it were capable of exact definition, and that ease of codability of each variation improved the recognition and later memory of that variation.

The name approach in teaching Doh or C

This approach has been found particularly popular with

children; everyone has a name, so also do sounds. The teacher can sing the child's name to the speech rhythm on the sound of C, while playing softly on the tone bar. In a group of children, the teacher can go round the whole group singing each child's name in turn to the sound of C. This is yet another instance of providing the repetition of one pitched sound while introducing something new.

When first names are being used and sung without difficulty, surnames can also be sung, and then both first names and surnames. These can lead on to the explanation that musical sounds also have two names, the first name only being used while we are small, in the same way that we use our first name every day leaving the surname for 'grown-up' occasions. The first note the child has learnt also has two names – Doh and C. Later on the child will learn that just as there are many people called Peter with different surnames, so there are many 'Dohs' with different second names. Initially, however, we shall keep to the sound of Doh for C to prevent confusion.

To introduce the concept of Doh and C, the teacher can play on the C tone bar and tune the voice by humming very softly. Gradually change from humming to singing 'Doh', alternating these. The child can then copy, which helps him to keep in tune, make a pleasant sound and learn the name of the sound he is making.

The child can then climb on to the first step of the ladder, and the teacher explains that when he stands on the first step of the musical ladder he must sing the name of the first step, Doh. This develops an understanding of the spatial aspect of pitch learning.

When this is clearly understood, the child can draw a picture of himself climbing on to the step of the musical ladder; when he sees this picture he must play on the C tone bar and sings its first name, Doh. For future practice he must begin by tuning his voice in the usual way by humming, and then from humming to singing Doh.

The next stage is for developing the idea of low-pitched sounds. Again this can be done by associating it with something the child can understand. I have found that names of parts of the body are useful for this. Even if the child is not yet fully aware of all the names, he needs to learn them, and by so doing will develop the body awareness necessary for spatial learning.

Start by teaching the child to touch his toes when singing Doh (remember that all movement stimulates eye muscle activity and permits spatial information to be fed back to the brain). Explain that just as his toes are at the bottom of his body, so Doh is at the bottom of the musical ladder. On the note of C the child can sing the words: 'We touch our toes when we sing 'Doh-Doh-Doh-Doh'. The teacher can play the note C as a signal for the child to sit down, using it at all times as a direction to sit down. Gradually reinforce the idea of Doh being a *low* note.

The idea of silence as a means of developing listening skills should be introduced as soon as possible. A simple method of doing this is to explain that the musical ladder has become very tired with so many people climbing on it and singing, it needs a rest. The sign for a rest ▬ can be put on the ladder for all to see, and in future when this sign  is sitting on the ladder the child must hold his forefinger to his lips and creep away softly to allow the ladder to have its rest. The more encouragement a child receives to pay attention to *silence* the greater the development of his discriminative ability. Codifying silence assists this attention.

The child can now draw a little 'rest' sign, colour it black and cut it out. Whenever the teacher wishes the child to be quiet. The teacher holds up the rest sign and the child puts his forefinger to his lips and remains very quiet. This a particularly a useful sign which can help considerably in the development of visually codifying sounds.

The 'Humpty Dumpty' approach in teaching Doh or C

Introducing the crotchet and minim beats

Codifying note duration can be approached through a story based on the nursery rhyme 'Humpty Dumpty'. This may seem rather a simplified idea to illustrate this point, but in the author's experience children identify quickly with the Humpty

Dumpty family. It can be used to introduce traditional notation by suggesting that Mr Humpty Dumpty looks like this: ♩ (a crotchet, or one beat); when he sits on the first step of the musical ladder he sings Doh. Mrs Humpty Dumpty, however, looks like this: ♩ (a minim, or two beats); when she sits on the first step of the musical ladder she sings Doh-oh, which is twice as long as when Mr Humpty Dumpty sings his Doh. The Humpty Dumpty theme is used throughout the book to illustrate duration.

The child should be encouraged to make a picture book of all the sounds learnt so far, drawing a separate picture for each of the different sounds he can make. Another approach is

for the teacher to 'allow' the child to teach her to play and sing the sounds of each picture. Try being a little slow to learn!

The shopping expedition

This game specifically draws attention to variations in tonal quality. All our speech sounds vary in tonal quality according to the shape, size and nature of the resonating cavity formed by the speech organs to produce each sound.

The teacher and children set out to buy all the things needed for their home on the first step of the musical ladder. So everything bought must be able to sing the sound of Doh while sitting on the first step of the musical ladder.

In this game, the teacher takes the xylophone round the classroom playing on it softly, while finding objects which, when banged or blown, produce the same sound as given by the xylophone. This provides a useful means of developing critical listening with variety. Kitchen utensils can produce various sounds. Bottles can be filled with water to the level at which the note of C is produced when the bottle is tapped by a spoon, etc. Sounds with saucepans, glasses, jugs and whisks can also be explored. Remembering to involve the child in all this, the teacher can collect as many environmental sounds as possible by recording them on the tape recorder, and selecting those with the sound of Doh. In this way the child gradually learns to listen critically. Later on, using these sounds, whole tunes can be composed.

Movement activities that can emphasize the duration aspect of sound include 'stretching out' for long sounds and 'curling up small' for short sounds. A picture of a snake slithering across the floor can be used for a long sound, or a snail for a short sound, and these can be acted out by the child either slithering or curling up before being added to the picture book.

Chapter Four

The Fourth Step

Hearing is considerably in advance of vocalization, and because of this and the limitations of the young child's vocal organs it is very important that activities do not impede learning.

The influence of vocalizing activities on pitch learning has been mentioned above, and there is a tendency to equate the two abilities. However, one has only to think of all the sounds that we can hear and yet not vocalize, to realize that activities bringing meaning to sounds which cannot be vocalized to aid learning are necessary, if the young child is to explore his full potential learning of sounds and their meanings. A study of phonation explains these limitations and, hopefully, will prevent the use of restrictive activities which suppress rather than promote full development.

Phonation

The process of phonation begins with an increase in electrical activity of the adductory muscles which reaches a maximum just before the onset of sound. From 0.35 to 0.55 sec is needed to build up the energy required to produce the sound. An increase in the volume of the sound causes no change in electrical activity, but with the rise in pitch there is an increase in activity indicating that the tension in the vocal cords is adjusted to a given pitch before the sound is actually produced. When the subject is asked to merely *think* about the production of a given pitched sound, without actually emitting the sound, the electrical activity increases.

The pitch of any sound is naturally controlled by the speed at which the sound is vibrating. This speed relies on the thickness and length of the vibrating object, as well as the amount of force applied to cause vibration. The smaller and shorter the object, the quicker the vibrating speed and therefore the higher the pitch sensation experienced.

The young child's larynx is very small. So learning to reproduce the correct kinaesthetic sensation involved in making a previously learnt pitched sound requires considerable experience of identical sensations as in any other first learning, and, as explained above, proceeds one note at a time (Figure 24).

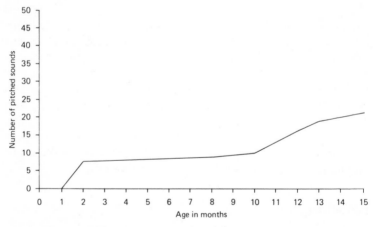

Figure 24 Pitch sounds vocalized by babies

The growth spurts of the young child's larynx is really placing the pre-6-year-old child in a similar position to that of the boy at puberty, in other words a constant state of change, perhaps instability, caused by a gradual increase in the length of the vocal folds. These lengths are: at 3 days, 3 mm; at 14 days, 4 mm; at 2 months, 5 mm; at 9 months, about 5.2 mm; at 1 year, 5.5 mm; at 5 years, 7.5 mm; at 6½ years, 8 mm; at 15 years, 9.5 mm; adult female, 12.5 to 17 mm; and, adult male, 17 to 23 mm. In the male there is a sudden increase in length at the time of puberty, with corresponding changes in the voice (Negus 1949).

If the child is not involved in the type of activity where he can constantly listen to sounds, he may well fail to learn to monitor the sounds made and to make the constant adjustments caused by the continually changing size of the larynx. This, however, can be avoided by playing many games involving individual sounds.

The vocal range of the child

The next note in the hierarchy of learning has been identified, by research as the note G.

The vocal range of the child is not the same as the auditory perceptual range. For every sound vocalized we must be able to experience the full range of harmonics, normally through our hearing which establishes the auditory feedback. This explains the need for the high frequencies and the resultant distortion of sounds when these are missing. According

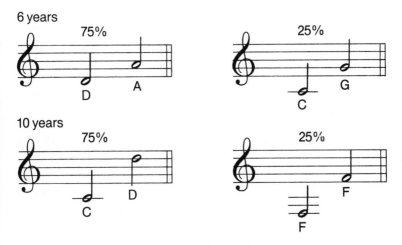

Figure 25 Development of the infantile vocal range for singing

to Sutzman (1907), the majority of children develop a vocal range of one-and-a-half octaves before puberty, with about 30% possessing approximately two octaves. According to Hell (1938) the infantile vocal range for singing develops as shown in Figure 25.

These vocal range limitations are supported by Jersild, Bienstock, Hartzell, Hathwick and Sherman. Imhofer (Zurich Medical School) has commented on on the unusually narrow vocal range found among the subnormal, implying that intelligence affects vocal range.

My work in a special school showed that intelligence affects pitch learning *after* puberty, but not before, and vocal range depends on vocal fold length and training, with every indication that the latter affects the vocal fold length by: (a) stimulating growth; and (b) gaining control in ability to vary vocal fold length. This aspect could be affected by intelligence, since gaining the control necessary to vary the vocal folds length at will requires the ability to relate sensations.

I have found a limited vocal range among tribes directly proportional to the exceptionally narrow range of their language, but in the case of very young children their experimental and exploratory vocalizing covered the same range of others, which, in my opinion, illustrates that range at least is partially dependent on development by use. It is conceivable, however, that since experiencing higher harmonics relies on auditory perception, which in turn must be learnt, the perceptually handicapped child could find this an additional problem which may well result in a limited vocal range. Perhaps this partly explains the improved overall performance when subnormal children are given hearing aids. A study of the vocal fold growth shows that the vocal folds are approximately 8 mm at 6½ years of age, and then remain stationary until a sudden increase at puberty.

If this is compared with the increased vocal range between 6 and 10 years of age it must surely confirm the effects of training on the development of vocal range. A study of the training programme used with children from the age of approximately 4 years upwards confirms the limitations of the vocal range according to Hell prior to training, with the exception that I have found only one child who started d° to a°, and she gained c° after 8 months.

In a project involving 115 children aged between 3 and 9 years, I found that they initially coped better with learning pitched sounds when these were approached by leaps instead of steps, until about the age of 8 years when this slowly began to change, possibly because increased vocal control made the production of smaller changes much easier. The other interesting difference was that individual efforts produced more accurate intonation than group work. This, however, began to change at about 7 years of age. Summarizing these points and relating them to the earlier description of the order in which children learn the pitched sounds, that is C and then G, identifies G as the next note to be learnt.

Teaching the sound of G or Soh

If the child can make the correct sound to be learnt without having to wait for an adult to identify this for him, the next step must be to teach the child how to do this, and at the same time, to aid discrimination introduce in a simple manner the spatial aspect of pitch learning. This can best be done by once again starting with a complete xylophone.

Leaving the C tone bar on the xylophone, the child can now remove the D, E and F tone bars; also leaving the G tone bar A, B and top C can also be removed.

This procedure can be practised several times, the child can quite readily produce the xylophone with only the G and C tone bars in position; its appearance, then, the teacher can tell the child, is just like a ladder with only two steps. In this way the child understands by implication that there is a gap between C and G that they are not directly next to each other.

To reinforce the idea of a ladder, the xylophone is held alongside a two-step ladder, previously cut out of cardboard; the teacher plays on the bottom tone bar of C, and at the same time points to the bottom step of the cardboard ladder. This is repeated with the G tone bar.

When experimenting with children between the ages of 2 and 3 years, I found that they had no difficulty in playing on the correct tone bar when a toy was placed on the corresponding position of the ladder, and the terminology of high/low and bottom/top was also gradually understood. A similar development in understanding symbolic representation did not begin until after the age of 3 years, and it was discovered that the best approach was through suitable nursery rhyme characters, or stories, such as Humpty Dumpty, which is used in this book. This nursery rhyme character is particularly suitable because it can eventually lead to both an understanding of traditional music notation and the provision of suitable symbols for the spatial training involved in reading.

The next pitched sound can be introduced by the following story. This step is important for the recognition of the small changes of pitch involved in continuing speech and localizing of sounds, and the type of game approach necessary is suggested, in the story below.

The Humpty Dumpty family visit Africa

The family are travelling by aeroplane all the way to Africa; a car takes them to the airport where they are to board their plane. This game needs both the C and the G tone bars on the xylophone. If the child has no toy motor car or a toy aeroplane models can be made from dough, clay or plasticine.

The teacher plays softly on the C tone bar while the car moves along taking the family to the airport; when the family are on the plane it then starts to take off for the journey to Africa. Continue playing on the C tone bar while the plane moves along the runway, and as it leaves the ground change to playing softly on the G tone bar, continuing on this note all the time the plane is in the air. This, of course, teaches the association between C as a low sound (while the plane is on the ground) and G as a higher sound while the plane is in the air; the sound of C is used for the plane as it comes down and lands on the runway in Africa.

Further understanding can be developed and practice given in localilzing sound sources and anticipation of spatial positions by encouraging children to run to the window to watch passing sound sources or overhead aircraft. This also enhances spatial learning and laterality training, which needs just as much repetition of experience as all other forms of first learning.

The story can then be repeated with the child acting out the movements, such as taking the family in his model car to the airport from where they will fly the plane to Africa. The teacher plays the sounds on the xylophone while the child copies the actions; later he can sing and play the sounds for himself while he makes the actions. In this way he is introduced to the idea of higher and lower sounds and to the next note for learning.

(Remember, this note is used because it appears to be the highest note that young children can control vocally, until they have had some practice in singing sounds to match those that they hear. Having such a small larynx they can happily screech very high sounds, but controlling the sound is a different matter; as with every activity requiring the control of muscles, this needs a great deal of practice before the correct control is obtained. This is particularly crucial during the spurts of growth of the child's larynx during early childhood, because, as explained above, it means that they must listen very carefully to their own attempts to match the sounds, as the vocalizing sensation varies with the growth of the larynx).

Introducing notation

The dotted minim

To introduce a longer note which looks like this: 𝅗𝅥. (dotted minim, or three beats) we can return to the Humpty Dumpty family; while on holiday in Africa they are fascinated by the manner in which the African mothers look after their babies. They visit an African village and watch the tiny babies being carried snug and comfortable on their mother's back. The mother would sing and dance all day long while she worked, and her baby could hear her singing and feel her moving to the sounds. The Humpty Dumpty family, however, did not like some of the songs because the notes seem to be repeated over and over again; they did not realize that this was just the African way of communicating, but they were very impressed by the way the very small children soon learnt to sing and dance so well.

When the Humpty Dumpty family are ready to return home, they once again go to the airport to board their plane for home. The child can now act out the journey home with his model car and aeroplane, playing and singing the sounds of both on the ground (the C tone bar), then the flight home (on the G tone bar), followed by the aircraft coming in to land (on the C tone bar).

Show the child pictures of African women carrying their babies on their backs; and demonstrate this by putting a small doll on the back of a larger doll, or letting the child carry his teddy, or doll on his own back.

All the above leads to the explanation that musical notes also carry their babies on their backs – like this ♩. When Mrs. Humpty Dumpty carried her baby on her back, she was of course much longer so she sang a longer sound, Doh-oh-oh, which is just half as long again as the sound she sang before her baby was born.

The Humpty Dumpty family now make three separate sounds when they each sit on the musical ladder.

Mr Humpty Dumpty sings Doh. ♪

Mrs Humpty Dumpty sings Doh-oh. ♩

Mrs Humpty Dumpty with her baby on her back sings Doh-oh-oh. ♩.

The semibreve

An even longer sound: 𝅝 (semibreve, or four beats) can be introduced through the character of Grandma Humpty Dumpty and the story continued as follows.

One day Grandma Humpty Dumpty decides that she would like to see her grandson. As she lives a long way away she is coming by plane so all the Humpty Dumpty family set off in their car to meet her at the airport. The child can drive his model car to the airport singing and playing the sound of C. Out of the car comes Mr Humpty Dumpty: *play and sing Doh.* ♩

Mr Humpty Dumpty then helps Mrs Humpty Dumpty out of the car: *play and sing Doh-oh.* ♩ Mrs Humpty Dumpty unstraps her baby from his carrycot and puts him on her back: *sing and play Doh-oh-oh.* ♩·

The child can play and sing on the G tone bar very softly, getting gradually louder and louder as the plane comes nearer and nearer. Play on the C tone bar for landing.

When the aircraft lands, the doors open and there is Grandma Humpty Dumpy: 𝅝 Although a little fatter she looks just like Mrs Humpty Dumpty but without her tail. (In the old days Grandpa and Grandma Humpty Dumpty did not grow tails as they had learnt to balance themselves properly without them).

All the Humpty Dumpty family now squeeze into their car and set off for their home on the musical ladder. There is:

Mr Humpty Dumpty – *play and sing Doh.* ♩

Mrs Humpty Dumpty – *play and sing Doh-oh.* ♩

Mrs Humpty Dumpty with her baby on her back – *play and sing Doh-oh-oh.* ♩·

and now there is also Grandma Humpty Dumpty – *play and sing Doh-oh-oh-oh.* 𝅝

The child can now make models and draw pictures of each member of the Humpty Dumpty family and practise singing their separate sounds of varying lengths while playing the C tone bar on the xylophone. (All the Humpty Dumpty family must, of course, tune their voices by humming to the note of C before singing!)

The quaver

Shortly baby Humpty Dumpty begins to crawl, so every now

and again he leaves his mother's back and crawls along the musical ladder. The baby's sound is the shortest sound of all and looks like this: ♪ (quaver, or half a beat). This sound can now be practised.

There are now five sounds of different durations starting with baby Humpty Dumpty's quaver to Grandma Humpty Dumpty's semibreve:

♪ ♩ Doh; ♩ Doh-oh; ♩. Doh-oh-oh; 𝅝 Doh-oh-oh-oh;

As the time approaches for Grandma Humpty Dumpty to return home she takes the baby to see the animals in the zoo, where they see the snakes with their long sounds — Doh-oh-oh-oh; tiny snails with their very short sound — Doh; in the aquarium they see a long crocodile — Doh-oh-oh-oh; and some very small tadpoles — Doh.

When Grandma Humpty Dumpty leaves the whole Humpty Dumpty family squeeze into their car and go to the airport. There is Mr Humpty Dumpty: ♩ Doh; Mrs Humpty Dumpty: ♩ Doh-oh; Grandma Humpty Dumpty: 𝅝 Doh-oh-oh-oh; and of course Baby Humpty Dumpty: ♪. When they reach the airport Mrs Humpty Dumpty puts the baby on her back so that he can wave to his Grandma: ♩. . Doh-oh-oh.

As the plane takes off, the teacher can play on the G tone bar while the child lifts his model plane in a simulated take-off. In this simple way, a story for children can be used to bring about an understanding and the use of traditional notation.

Pitch learning

The learning of pitch is essential to the individual, as it has been shown to have great influence on the standard of learning eventually achieved. I suggest that importance for young children is based initially on basic survival rather than aesthetic needs, and that this importance must be demonstrated during the early childhood years when sensory acuity coexists with neural plasticity. In this way potential learning can be maximized.

I formed the hypothesis that any early childhood environment requiring great pitch discrimination for basic survival should result in greater pitch learning. I selected two possible situations where pitch, discrimination and memory would have great importance for basic survival purposes, and then compared their learning with that of other groups. The first example was that of the tonal speaking groups where meaning is based on the pitch of the vowel entoned, and the second example was where children were born blind and relied on pitch for information about their immediate environment.

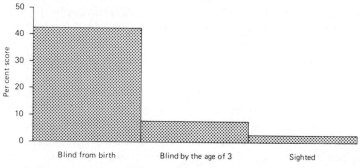

Figure 26 Comparing the absolute pitch acquisition of children born blind, with normal sight and with acquired blindness (in Europe)

Those taking part in this test included 500 sighted mixed ability, children from a comprehensive school, and 500 blind and partially sighted mixed ability children from schools of the blind. Audiological screening showed them to be within the normal range, in other words the audiometer was set at 20 dB, and screening was carried out by sweep through 250 Hz, 1000 Hz, 4000 Hz and 8000 Hz.

Figure 26 shows that of the children who were born blind and relied on pitch discrimination during the first 3 years of life for information about their surrounding environment, about 42% had acquired absolute pitch. Those going blind after the age of 3 were, as a group, still in advance of the normally sighted child, but showed a dramatic drop in the absolute pitch learning. With the normally sighted group only one child has acquired absolute pitch.

In an experiment designed to assess the incidence of absolute pitch in a normal European community, I tested (at the piano) 1120 children between the ages of 8 and 12 using Girl Guide and Brownie packs in the Home Counties around London. The children were neither screened audiologically nor assessed for IQ, and sixteen were found to have acquired absolute pitch, accurate to within a semitone, at least nine times out of every ten tests.

Approximately one child in every 70, or decimally 0.014, children, of the normal European community were found to possess absolute pitch.

Exploring this further, I found the following facts, as shown in Table 2 below.

Table 2

Total children tested	Instruments played by child				Parents played	Absolute pitch learnt	Sang in tune	Read music
	Wind	Violin	Guitar	Piano				
1120	538	73	99	162	205	16	624	478

The sixteen absolute pitch subjects also had in common:

(1) they all played the piano;

(2) they all had parents or relatives living in the house who played an instrument;

(3) they all sang in tune to an instrument (even when the instrument was out of tune); at this stage they were able to vary pitch slightly;

(4) fourteen of them read music fluently; two of them repeated phrases at the exact pitch a week later, and were thus assessed as having absolute pitch although they could not actually name the notes.

General observations

(1) Of the 1120 children tested the greater number (538) played wind instruments, mainly the recorder; of these only

three acquired absolute pitch and each also played the piano. No child playing a wind instrument on its own had acquired absolute pitch.

(2) In the same group of 1120 children, 73 played the violin; eight of these had acquired absolute pitch, but again they had also learnt to play the piano.

(3) None of the children learning the guitar had acquired absolute pitch.

(4) Whereas all sixteen children who had acquired absolute pitch had parents and/or relatives playing an instrument in the immediate environment, a further 189 children also had parents who played an instrument, yet they failed to learn absolute pitch. Additionally, 462 could read music, 608 sing in tune, 146 play the piano, all without acquiring absolute pitch.

Acquisition of pitch by tonal and non-tonal-speaking groups in Africa

In European languages the vowel sounds tend to be the least critical features and a considerable frequency range is tolerated. The pitch of a voiced sound is raised or lowered by increasing or decreasing the contraction of the vocal cords. If therefore, changes of pitch within vowel sounds are not critical, the purpose of training a child to speak will not involve the reinforcement of the 'quantitatively exact responses' of the vocal cords to the frequency changes needed for singing in tune. There are, however, many languages in which the meanings of words are largely dependent on intonation of the voiced sounds, so the child must learn to determine the tension of the vocal cords in order to communicate. It is significant that so-called tone deafness in the absence of physiological defects is virtually unknown in tonal-speaking communities using such a language.

In order to observe the early training of the young in both tonal and non-tonal-speaking tribes, I spent almost 2 years 'in the bush' observing and recording the methods of training the children and the resultant progress. I collected material and tested some 97 different tribal groups in South Africa,

Botswana, Zimbabwe-Rhodesia, Zambia, Swaziland, and Lesotho, working with both tonal and non-tonal speaking groups.

I noticed in general that there was little difference in a baby's response to sound during the first 6 to 8 months of age from those I had observed in England. Babbling developed in the same way, and there was no evidence of any greater acuity of hearing or special facility for pitch learning than in the European children, but when the African children started to experiment with more than one sound and form speech sounds there appeared to be a far greater attention to the pitch of each sound. This, however only appeared to result from the mother's attention to pitch, as she was teaching the child throughout the day, constantly repeating very small phrases. There was no doubt that the children were learning absolute pitch for the following reasons:

(1) the language demanded it;
(2) a great deal of practice went into satisfying the demands of the language;
(3) a far smaller vocal range was initially explored.

The material collected all supported the finding that, regardless of race, if pitch training took place in pre-puberty years then it was successful in establishing a pitch memory, and the earlier the training began the more positive was the learning of absolute pitch. The work was carried out with the assistance of the Department of African Languages, Cape Town University; Groote Schuur Hospital; Tigerberg Hospital; Johannesburg Hospital; Speech and Hearing Clinic, Pretoria; and Harari Hospital. The broadcasting stations in Lesotho, Zambia, Swaziland, Botswana, and Zimbabwe-Rhodesia kindly assisted with recordings. His Majesty Sobbluzu II, King of Swaziland, generously gave me permission to make recordings of traditional music in Swaziland. The Needler Westdene Hearing Organization were most helpful in loaning equipment. Many tribal chiefs, mission hospitals and schools assisted in the collection of materials and the Meat Marketing Board often provided transport to remote areas.

A total of 11 120 children were tested; 10 000 in Africa and 1120 in England. Testing was carried out by teaching melodies and then checking over a period (with a tape recorder) the ability to sing from memory at the exact pitch. The accuracy of the tape recorder was governed by the use of a sound level indicator and pitch meter. The tunes were first collected from the village elders (the actual tune used when working with the Bemba tribe is shown below, Figure 27), and using music belonging to each tribe was to ensure equal scoring opportunities.

Figure 27 Bemba tunes

Research showed that in spite of the very high incidence of damage to hearing from disease, malnutrition, insects, etc., the tonal speakers of Africa were considerably in advance of the European children in that some 85% appeared to have absolute pitch as against 0.06% of the European population (Figure 28). Somewhat surprisingly the non-tonal tribes also had a relatively high standard of absolute pitch learning, approximately 42%. This would appear to be as a result of early involvement, as I noticed that all children until they could walk were carried on their mothers' backs all day even during the dancing and singing, which took up a major part of their time.

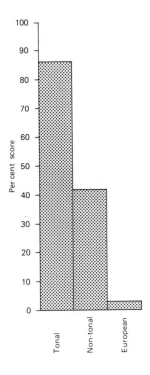

Figure 28

Every basic function of life was expressed in singing and dancing and a great deal of practice went into this. In many of these groups dancing, singing, gesture and speech were all described as language. A number of psychologists have claimed that the limited vocabulary of these tribes must effectively limit their intellectual development, but the former have obviously failed to understand how the vocabulary is extended via pitch variation of the vowels, dance, gesture, mime, drumming, etc. to a very broad vocabulary which is completely adequate for even the greatest intellectual development. They sang and danced about the basic functions of life, such as washing their faces, to the great dramas of childbirth, circumcision, puberty, marriage, war, love, etc. Pitch was used to express extremes of emotion at this basic functional level which contributed to the degree of pitch perception shown by even the non-tonal-speaking tribes. As mentioned above, babies were involved in this from birth because until they were able to walk they were physically carried by their mothers constantly, therefore gaining maximum auditory stimulation during their optimum years for learning sounds (shown as pre-puberty years in Figure 29 below). I disagree, however, with Whetnell and Fry when they show that the maximum facility in learning to recognize new sounds only develops from 3 years. In my opinion this facility is present from birth in all normal children, and then gradually drops from the age of 3.

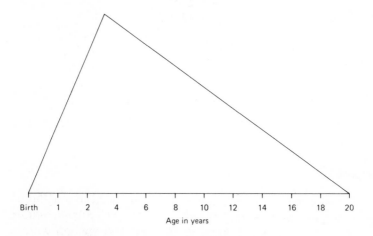

Figure 29 Facility for learning to recognize new sounds in children (according to Whetnell and Fry)

At Bulawayo Music College I noticed how quickly Africans learnt tonic solfa, the idea of pitched vowel sounds being part of their language. The Principal of the College told me of missionaries who taught hymns with conventional tunes, but translated the words into traditional language, failing to understand that the variation of meaning according to pitch made nonsense of the hymns. This highly amused the Africans.

It is possible that even with the non-tonal African tribes, the nature of their language helps in pitch learning since each vowel sound is clearly enunciated and pronounced as it written (the vowel sounds even in non-tonal languages are likened to musical chords). The Italian language, is a European equivalent, which perhaps explains the remarkable number of excellent Italian singers. Remembering that musical sounds are perceived as louder than non-musical, any language demanding clear vowel enunciation would assist pitch learning.

The pitch of a sound depends mainly on the fundamental frequency, so when there is a variation in the rate at which pulses are produced by the vocal cords there will be a change in the pitch, although no change in the formants or the chord quality. According to Ladefoged (1962) in 'musical terms you can say, corresponding to each vowel there is a chord that is characteristic of that vowel'.

The relationship between learning and need is further illustrated by the way the baby responds to the 'need' sounds first, such as preparation of food, mother's voice, etc. A study of the growth of word classes provides further illustration since it can be seen that the 'need' words (nouns) are the first to be learnt, with verbs, the next 'need' words, being the second to be learnt, and so on.

Age in years and months	Nouns	Verbs	Adjectives	Adverbs	Prepositions	Pronouns	Conjunctions
1 year	4	1					
1 year and 2 months	15	1	1	1			
1 year and 4 months	39	6	2	2	4		
1 year and 6 months	80	12	9	3	4		
1 year and 9 months	193	51	28	7	7	1	
2 years	349	111	58	7	11	8	1
2 years and 6 months	410	140	85	25	12	13	8
3 years	571	201	129	53	23	17	11

A suitable study of this was made by Valentine, Kellner, Pringle and Tanner in 1942.

Studies with the progeny of musicians

I found two contrasting situations of study, one where the daughter of a composer had developed a love of music, so her child was surrounded by music from birth, and another whose son was tired of a household revolving around music, so his children apparently heard little music at home. The grandchild of the first musician had a very good sense of absolute pitch, but neither of the second composer's grandchildren could cope even with the simple tests of relative pitch at the age of 14. This would support the view that the availability of music in the early environment has greater influence than innate ability on acquiring absolute pitch.

In Desmond Sergeant's work the effect of parental ability to play an instrument on pitch learning is shown graphically. With both parents playing, the score was 35.3%; with the mother only playing it was 30.4%, and with the father only playing it was 13.5%. Again this stresses the *immediate* environment at the optimum age, since the mother is normally at home playing the piano while the young child too is at home. At least one parent played an instrument in 79.2% cases. The immediate environment as opposed to inherent ability aspects are once again emphasized in a statistical study of (Schuter, 1969) absolute pitch progeny of parents as musicians. In this case 11.2% of the parents who were professional musicians were mothers, and 10% were fathers, so in slightly over 21% one parent or the other was a professional musician, but slightly less than 79% had neither. I suggest that this further indicates that it is the constant musical environment rather than any sex differential which affects hereditary traits. The large percentage with neither parent as a professional musician further illustrates the value of evoked response and training, since in my experience I have found that whereas a child hears plenty of instrumental practice and performance from the parents when they are professional musicians, they rarely have the benefit of a sensibly planned training to meet their own development needs (see Justine Ward's work on the kind of music teacher required in the primary school). The children frequently tend to reject the music made by their professional musician parents if it appears to be, in the child's opinion, more important to the parent than the child, rejection is clearly a barrier to learning.

The importance of the immediate environment in learning through hearing is further illustrated by the number of children with 'learnt' speech defects; here children whose speech seemed to be the result of a high frequency deafness were tested by routine pure tone audiometry, and found to have no such hearing loss. In each case though one parent had such a hearing loss and the child appeared to have 'learnt' the defective speech. It is therefore imperative that the young child is afforded the maximum opportunity to experience and so learn all aspects of sound.

Further exercises and games

A version of 'musical chairs' can be played to reinforce the understanding of high and low. While the teacher plays on the C tone bar of the xylophone the child runs around the room, but when the G tone bar is played then the child sits on a chair, form or stool.

Another exercise to help develop foot/eye coordination and stimulate the use of the eyes can develop from this. The teacher can balance a plank of wood on two objects, one at each end, or, if this is not possible, use a form. While she plays the C tone bar on the xylophone the child stands on the floor, but when the G tone bar is played he must jump on the plank or form. Balancing on the form can be developed by playing various styles of music for walking, running, or jumping, etc. along the form.

If the child has difficulty in keeping his balance, he should be examined by an orthoptist at the nearest eye hospital. He may be having difficulty in making the necessary fine ocular muscle adjustments even though his visual acuity is quite normal in both eyes when examined uniocularly. A good way of finding out about this is for the child to close his eyes and repeat the activities, relying only on just feeling his way along. If this produces better results than when he had his eyes open, then his eyes and vestibular system must be examined as soon as possible; if results are poor, vestibular function should still be checked.

Another game to develop sensitive listening while demonstrating how much the young child is able to learn through his ability to hear is for the teacher to ask him to close his eyes and listen to any movements she makes, for instance, walking, running, hopping and skipping. Then ask him to open his eyes and repeat the same movements.

To reinforce the constant repetition necessary for learning, the teacher can explain to the child that he must now tune his voice to the sounds of both steps, C and G, singing the first name of each sound, Doh while playing C, and Soh when playing G.

All the games that were played in the note of C should also be played using the new note G. As young children learn one sound at a time, the new sound must be practised often, and great care taken not to move on to the new material too quickly. If the first sound took a month to learn the new sound will take almost as long. Progress should become faster as the child learns to listen.

Another important point is that because the young child's brain is so very pliable it is necessary to remind him constantly over maybe a year of what he has already learnt. Each daily session can be a 'learning sandwich', starting with the new material to be learnt, playing one or two games using the old material and then returning to the new material. In this way learning becomes stabilized and eventually reasonably permanent.

Picture activities

Any pictures drawn at this stage should include the sound of the higher step of the musical ladder, called Soh. A model of a cat sitting on the higher step of the ladder would sing 'me-ow' on G (Soh). This is 'Soh' having a rest. The child must hold his fingers to his lips and creep softly away.

Go through all the pictures of the sounds in the first few chapters and draw them sitting on the G step of the musical ladder singing Soh. For each picture practise singing and playing the sound; new games to demonstrate the higher pitch of the sound of G can also be played. Teach the child to touch his waist when he sings Soh and to touch his toes when singing Doh (see Chapter 5).

Another simple activity to demonstrate this point is to use the sound of G as a signal for the child to stand. This means that he must sit down on hearing C (Doh), stand up when he hears G (Soh), and put his fingers to his lips and be quiet when he sees the rest sign ▬ .

Yet another game that can be played for the middle part of the 'learning sandwich' is 'Pass the Parcel', to the sound of first Doh and then Soh. The child can make drawings on five separate cards, each representing a member of the Humpty Dumpty family.

Card 1

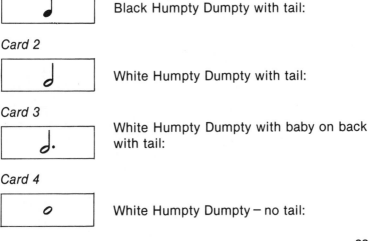

Black Humpty Dumpty with tail:

Card 2

White Humpty Dumpty with tail:

Card 3

White Humpty Dumpty with baby on back with tail:

Card 4

White Humpty Dumpty – no tail:

Card 5

 Black Humpty Dumpty with a very small and curly tail:

Make up a parcel with several layers of paper, placing a card between each layer. Arrange the children in a circle and let them pass the parcel to each other when the music starts. When the music stops the child holding the parcel unwraps the first layer of paper, takes out the first card, and sings the correct sound to match the picture, with no help from the tone bar. The music being played during the passing of the parcel can be either C (the child sings Doh) or G (the child sings Soh).

A playground swing can also be used to help the development of a child's spatial awareness, and as he swings, provide practice in the use of his eyes. The child can sing Soh as he swings up, and Doh as he comes down.

For 'musical bumps' the teacher can play on the G tone bar of the xylophone for the child to run around but as soon as C is played he must stop and sit down. This is also a very good game to play with a group of children where the last child to sit down is considered to be out of the game. When only one child remains standing and is declared the winner, his prize can be to take over the playing of the xylophone, and the game continues.

Chapter Five

The Fifth Step

As I explained above the first note that children appear to learn through their hearing is the note of C. Once the memory of this pitched note has become firmly enough established to be used for a fixed reference point, then spatial learning for both auditory span and frequency discrimination can really begin. We tend to forget that whereas the environment normally provides *visual* objects to use as reference points, and assist the development of visual function and spatial learning, for hearing the memory provides this; often there is an immediate improvement in clarity of speech once a hearing-impaired child has built up a memory of middle C.

The order in which children learn pitched sounds appears to follow a regular pattern. This was confirmed by some general observations noted during a training programme developed over a period of 10 years with 100 children. Again, as a result of trial and error, it was found that the best starting point for pitch training was middle C. In 3000 children tested I found only one variation. The pattern of progress which developed was as shown below.

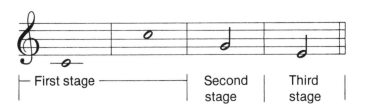

⊢ First stage ────────────⊣ Second stage ⊣ Third stage ⊣

At this stage D, F and A followed, but appeared to be learnt as a step from, or towards, one of the four previous notes. The 7th or final note (B) seemed to be more difficult to memorize, and was more easily learnt by the interval:

It was described by the children as 'standing out like a sore thumb'. Pitch learning at this stage meant the ability to listen to the given note and then play it correctly on a pitched instrument, singing it in tune to the correct name.

Care was taken to avoid the impression of testing for pitch memory, as apparently the too early testing which forms most of the aural training in schools causes lack of confidence by drawing attention to the intangibility of sounds before they are learnt. Once diatonic intervals are known, usually after a year, it is safe to progress to the introduction of the two accidentals mentioned and the idea of the movable Doh.

When this is established the teacher can proceed to modulation (using a note to change to a new key) and to the introduction of the minor key or mode. This must, however, be gradual as there is considerable evidence to suggest that work in minor keys is related to uncertainty.

The minor mode

Three simple examples illustrate the apparent lack of definition in the minor key, although controlled experiments were not possible.

(1) A group of 22 children was told to listen to two pieces of music on different afternoons, one in a major mode and the other in a minor. They were then asked to draw or paint

anything they liked which they felt fitted in with the music. Generally the major key music brought out brightly coloured, clearly defined paintings, while the minor key produced pallid, ephemeral paintings.

(2) In a school for emotionally disturbed children, the use of the minor keys had to discontinued with the younger children, because of the uncertainty and emotional disturbance it created regularly.

(3) A recording of a series of music therapy sessions with a patient in a psychiatric hospital illustrated his state of security. As he progressed towards being discharged his improvizing showed a moving away from the minor mode to the major. Later, having regressed, he returned to the hospital, and his improvization was back in the minor mode.

Introducing E (Me) and A (Lah) with the musical ladder

The musical ladder can be used as a vertical way to teach the lines and spaces of notation. The next step, E (or Me) can now be added to the musical ladder. The tone bar with the letter E on it is placed on the xylophone in between the tone bars C and G; the child can now draw a musical ladder with three steps. The teacher then plays softly in the middle of the E tone bar, tuning the voice by humming and singing alternately to this new sound of Me. The child can then copy this.

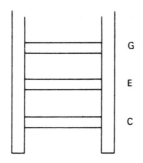

To introduce A or Lah, the teacher places the tone bar with A on it on the xylophone next to and above the G tone bar.

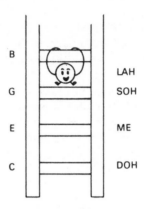

Resuming the Humpty Dumpty story can once again illustrate this. There are now four rungs or steps on the ladder but this time the Humpty Dumpty family cannot sit on the steps; to sing Lah they must swing from the step above, which is B. This teaches the first space note, A or Lah, and learning other sounds that 'swing in the space between the rungs or steps of the ladder can follow. The musical ladder now no longer looks exactly like the xylophone. The order in which sounds are introduced has been established through many years of research, as mentioned above in this chapter.

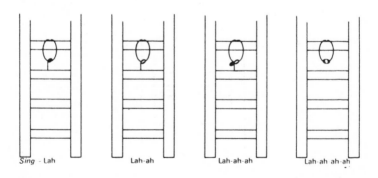

A climbing frame in the children's playground can also help the learning of Lah, as the child can try swinging from the rungs, 'just like the Humpty Dumpty family do'.

Using a piano the teacher can tune her voice to A on it, singing Lah. All the notes learnt so far can be played on both the piano and the xylophone. (In the absence of a piano a xylophone only should be used.)

To reinforce learning the child can now sing the sounds for the parts of the body, touching the correct part of the body as each sound is made. This establishes body awareness as spatial awareness can only develop after this stage.

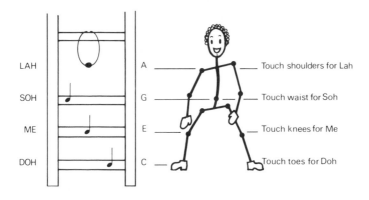

All the games previously played on the notes of C, G and E can now be played on the note of A.

Wherever possible other musical instruments should be used as it has been shown (Karlovich, 1968) how the visual, tactile and motor appeal of instruments are important factors in the later identification of their tone.

Many workers such as du Preez, Taylor, and Leontov have demonstrated the relationship between tonal awareness and language development. Du Preez describes the tone as providing information that aids the child's development from 'words' to complete 'sentences'. He shows that the child imitates the adult tonal centre, gradually increasing the length of utterances by adding the next salient note ('word') to the tonic.

Similarly Sergeant (1969) found that the learning of pitched sounds spread outwards from those already established. This observed behaviour appears to result from the children using their memory of these sounds as reference points; young children use this sense of tonality as a means of reproducing correct grammatical language. The tone colour, or timbre, of a note produced on a variety of instruments may so capture the focal point of a child's attention that learning will be enhanced. As Penfield continually stressed a child is only capable of remembering those things to which he pays sufficient attention, so the use of a variety of instruments to attract greater attention should therefore be explored.

It can be pointed out at this stage that all the players in an orchestra tune their instruments to the sound of A before playing any piece of music. When listening to a concert broadcast on the television or radio tune in both xylophone and voice to the note A. Another idea is to tape record the members of an orchestra tuning their instruments while the child listens too. The recording can then be used to add interest to the teacher's own tuning sessions.

Watching and listening to instruments being played develops the child's ability to recognize their various tonal qualities. Television performances are particularly good for this because the child can tune in with his own instrument and learn to mime playing other instruments, which can be used later to determine recognition of the various instruments. *Peter and the Wolf* in particular is excellent for recognizing tonal quality, and drawing pictures and making models of the figures in the story increases the memory span of the sounds. In the same way that musical instruments vary in tonal quality, so vowel sounds are really musical chords also varying in tonal quality. This is why any musical activities involving sounds of varying pitch, tonal quality, duration and intensity levels are so important in pre-literacy auditory training.

Introducing top C' (Doh')

The next new note, top C – Doh' (usually written as C´ or Doh') also swings from a step instead of sitting on it. The top C tone bar should be placed next door but one to A on the xylophone.

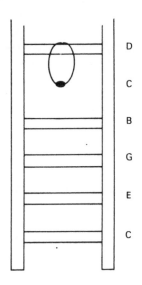

The teacher then plays softly on the tone bar, tuning her voice ready to sing the names of the sounds learnt so far, while touching the part of the body representing that sound.

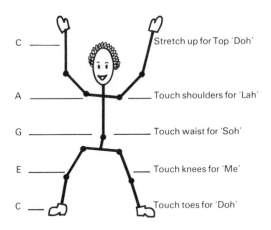

107

Top C is usually learnt more quickly than the others, but the eventual standard should not be spoilt by moving on too quickly.

By now a teacher will probably have spent about 8 months on these activities. If it is less, possibly she is moving too quickly. If it has taken longer, maybe she has been very thorough, or the child has needed extra opportunities to learn because of a hearing deficiency. A hearing-impaired child may take well over a year to reach this stage, but once he can monitor his voice to a pitched sound his speech clarity improves out of all recognition. There is a tendency in the education of the deaf to concentrate only on loudness levels, whereas it is the ability to *hear changes in frequency* that is so important.

All the games played previously can now be played on this new note. The Humpty Dumpty family and all the animals used can play and sing the new sound, and stories can be made up to illustrate this. The child should be constantly involved critically listening to pitched sounds of varying tonal quality, duration patterns and intensity levels, and surrounded by interesting, meaningful sounds to be learnt. If should not be forgotten that, although our hearing is much more advanced at birth, how much better we become at learning through our visual system as so many meaningful objects are visually around us all day long just waiting to be learnt.

Introducing D or Ray

To teach D or Ray, the tone bar D on it should be placed on the xylophone next to the very first note learnt, C. The voice on this sound is tuned by humming in the usual way and then gradually changing to singing Ray, with the child copying. As this note also swings in the space between two steps, Mr Humpty Dumpty can be drawn swinging by his tail from the E step of the ladder while D or Ray is played. The child can now add this picture to his collection.

The new note of D or Ray belongs to the shins, half way between the toes and knees on our musical body, which now looks like this.

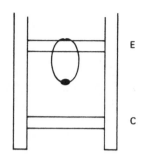

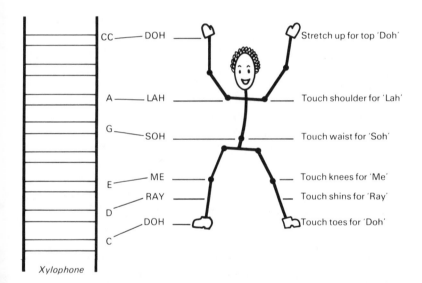

Xylophone

The child can now try touching the body singing the sound indicated by each part of the body touched, moving each time from C (Doh), and tuning in first.

> Doh up to Ray
> Doh up to Me
> Doh up to Soh
> Doh up to Lah
> Doh up to Top Doh′

The teacher can then try playing the sounds, with the child touching the correct part of his body for the note played. As the game progresses the notes can be played in any order and memory span increased. The need to increase auditory span is one of the greatest problems in remedial work and takes the longest time to rectify. This is because there is little establishment of a fixed reference point through building up the memory of one pitched sound. Span cannot be increased, or any spatial or sequential learning take place, until there is an act of comparison. The transient, ephemeral nature of sound prevents the environment from providing lifelong reference points for temporal skills, so the memory must make such provision.

Introducing F or Fah

To teach F or Fah the tone bar with F on it should be placed on the xylophone in between tone bars E and G; the new sound can be tuned into in the usual way, gradually changing to Fah.

F or Fah also swings in a space between steps of the ladder instead of sitting on a step, between G (Soh) and E (Me). Mr Humpty Dumpty can be drawn swinging by his tail from the G step of the ladder, and the child can add this picture to his collection. The part of the body used to indicate this sound is the thigh.

The teacher can now practise playing and singing all the sounds, touching the correct part of the body, with the child (and all the Humpty Dumpty family!) doing this.

Once again, all the games played on the other sounds can be repeated using the new note of F or Fah. When this new note has been learnt the teacher can move on to some well-known tunes, such as *Three Blind Mice*.

The C line is only drawn when it is actually required for a tune, which should be memorized to tonic solfa.

Introducing B or Te

The final sound to be learnt to complete the musical ladder is called Te or B. For this note the tone bar B is placed on the xylophone between tone bars A and top C′. The note B or Te sits on the step of the ladder above G. The teacher can tune her voice to Te (and make sure all the Humpty family can sing Te). The head on the musical body is used for this sound.

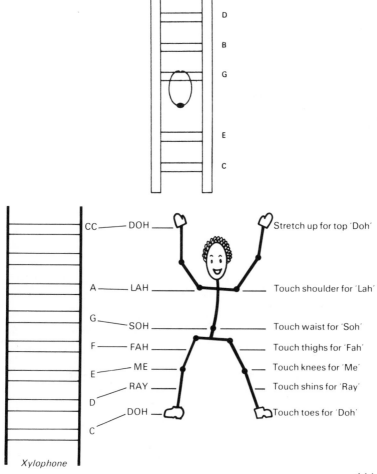

Xylophone

111

Learning the difference between long and short sounds

When the complete diatonic scale of pitched sounds has been learnt, the child is well on the way to the fine discrimination needed eventually for accurate spelling, and work can begin on blending together the auditory components that make up the speech sounds. Their visual symbolizing or codifying should also be continued and more specific hand/eye coordination developed. Learning the shortest sound can be illustrated once again by the Humpty Dumpty family, in this case Baby Humpty Dumpty who is now old enough to play on his own instead of spending all day on his mother's back. He can practise singing his very short sounds on each step of the ladder.

Very short and very long sounds of exactly the same pitch often sound quite different, and these must also be experienced and learnt; before they can be either codified or decodified they must be recognized in language.

A recorder or homemade bamboo pipe is particularly useful for learning the difference between very long and very short sounds; the advantages of the homemade pipe over the recorder is that the child can learn to produce a pleasant sound before having to worry about keeping his small fingers covering the holes of the pipe (these need not be made until the child is ready for this stage). Another advantage of playing a blown instrument is the increased oxygen intake that this activity stimulates, and visual convergence and finger control is also helped. The Guild of Pipe Makers provide simple instructions for making these instruments.

When the child can play both very short and very long sounds, picture cards can be introduced, Baby Humpty Dumpty representing the shortest possible sound ♪ , and Grandma Humpty Dumpty the longest sound 𝑜 . When the teacher holds up each card in turn the child must blow the correct length of sound. He can also draw a Baby Humpty Dumpty or a Grandma Humpty Dumpty when the teacher plays the length of sound that each represents to gradually develop the memory of these sounds and extend the memory span of their patterns. For example:

♪♪♪ ○ equals three short blows and one very long blow.

The child should be encouraged both to copy the patterns by playing his own pipes and then to draw the notes. The teacher can then draw patterns of sounds and ask the child to play them. For example:

(1) ♪♪○

(2) ○♪♪

(3) ○♪♪♪

(4) ♪○♪

Movement in time to the music of course further increases learning, and this should be developed into an awareness of rhythmic stress by playing, for example, a march (counting 1, 2, 3, 4 or 1, 2) or a waltz (counting 1, 2, 3) or skipping music, stressing the beat. Playing and singing tunes with the correct accent on the beat is valuable preparation for recognizing stress patterns in language; the child should be encouraged to recognize the stress sign above the music. Later this skill can be used for stressing the difference between long and short vowels.

Chapter Six

'And so to Literacy'

This chapter should be used more as a collection of ideas to handle specific problems than as a remedial training programme.

As a result of constant repetition of the components of language over at least a year, the child should now have the basic memory of those upon which functional literacy is based. If progress towards this stage has been too quick, for whatever reason, this basic memory will not be sufficiently established for either reliability or immediacy of response. Remember, that until a reference point has been firmly established in the memory, neither the act of comparison that becomes discrimination, nor spatial learning, can begin to develop. The eventual retention of learning, that in future should only require minimal reinforcement, will also be affected. As mentioned above, formal spelling, writing and reading is really blending together and organizing all the previous learning into spatial patterns of sounds and symbols. These skills are therefore totally dependent on this consistent learning.

When the child can easily produce the correct picture to identify sound by its pitch and tonal quality, as in identifying different instrumental sounds, or in rehearsal of the 'animal choir', he can then move on to a comparison of the language sounds. These vary not only in pitch and tonal quality but also contain several pitched sounds as in a chord. In spite of this, this complex mixture must be immediately analysed and the speech sound identified. No wonder such efficient learning of all the ingredients is required.

The animal stories illustrated by tape-recorded animal sounds, as discussed above, can now be used to test whether there has been sufficient learning to discriminate between all the many pitched sounds that make up language. (They can also be used as a basis for nature study or geography, as a study of bird songs and animal sounds can lead to an investigation of their habitat—every area of study and human knowledge is in fact an opportunity for developing literacy). Too often we only pay attention to the grading of vocabulary during so-called 'reading' lessons, when every area of study involves the study of words, which is the codifying and decodifying of complex sounds blended together and organized into spatial patterns.

It cannot be stressed too much that the accurate codifying of each pitched sound, with its many variations in tonal quality, which is the beginning of learning to spell, depends very largely on the availability of consistent sensitivity of hearing for the whole range of the sounds involved. This is normally available during very early childhood provided that there is no hearing impediment. It must not be forgotten, however, that even the slightest catarrhal cold or similar condition that blocks the small passages to hearing could interfere with this sensitivity. Even if a child outgrows this problem or receives suitable medical treatment, it could mean that although he has missed the initial chance to learn these sound ingredients and develop all other responses to sounds, he is now expected to use the memory of them to identify the language sounds and produce mature, learnt responses.

Musical activities, however, give these children a second chance to learn them. When the sounds have been codified, then and only then can they be decodified, in other words the representing symbol can be used to recall the sound from memory. This is the first stage of reading, although the recalling of the speech sound codified by the symbols of language has sometimes been called 'mere barking at print' and not reading. However, the next stage of being able to read with understanding and fluency cannot be reached until the 'barking' stage has been passed, although, constant attention must be given to the collection of meaning in order to progress to understanding.

Handwriting too involves both skills in addition to other skills. The kinaesthetic memory and motor control necessary to establish the required feedback system capable. of the necessary monitoring is the first essential. This monitoring includes the production of spatially organized patterns of symbols used in the codifying and decodifying processes.

As thousands of repetitions of sound codifying are necessary for learning, many children, once they are capable of hearing and seeing normally, needlessly fail because they do not receive sufficient repetition. Sound learning, because of its transient nature, needs even more repetition than visual learning. If one forgets the look of a visual shape or object, provided that the eye muscles can pull those 'little tunnels of vision' to fixate at the correct distance and visual acuity is normal, one can always have another look. Even if vision is subnormal, one can collect information about the object by feeling and touching, so making possible constant reinforcement and learning. If, however, a sound is forgotten it is not possible to have 'another look' as sound only exists while it is being made, so every skill involving sound is dependent on memory. Consequently, a child's development of language is dependent on the provision of sufficient and suitable opportunities to hear and thus develop a memory of the sounds required, or their codifying by visual objects is not possible.

One indication of insufficient experience is where the child finds it helpful to 'mouth the words' when attempting to decodify. This reduces the reading speed and is sometimes dealt with by artificially stimulating the speed of eye movement; if this is done, where sounds have received insufficient practice, inaccurate and careless reading can develop. A correctly positioned visual image on both retinas of the eyes simultaneously, so that the correct spatial information can be fed back to the brain, is dependent on the maturity and balance of eye muscle development; constant provision of this over the first 5 or 6 years of life makes possible efficient learning. Like all other muscles, the eye muscles require considerable use before coordination and control develops. A baby boy can hardly immediately play a skilled game of football, or a baby girl dance a complex ballet.

Similarly, the eye muscles need to be trained for the highly skilled and unnatural eye muscle activity involved in literacy. Initially a child's eyes are slightly divergent when at rest. The natural movement of the hands is to follow this direction, so both hands and eyes work from the centre outwards. Literacy skills require both eyes to fixate on the same object and to fuse both retinal images together; they must therefore receive practice in this convergent movement. In a child this usually develops as a result of the search for information about the world around him, stimulated by seeking out a sound source.

Once the child can easily seek out a sound source with his eyes, he must learn to hold both eyes in that position while making the small adjustments necessary to follow the sound. To learn to read, the child must then practise holding this position while it moves both eyes together from left to right; and when writing, both hands must also be trained to move from left to right. As this movement of the left hand in this direction is against natural movement a great deal of practice is required.

Frequently, a child does not receive sufficient practice to move both hands and eyes together in the correct direction, so the ability to reproduce spatially organized patterns of visual symbols is undeveloped. Left-handed children appear to need a year longer to establish hand/eye coordination, possibly because the world seems designed for right-handed people so the child misses the required opportunities to develop this coordination. Encouraging left-handed children to use their right hand as much as possible is, in my opinion, likely to hamper the development of a stable hand/eye relationship needed for literacy. Much needed training can be carried out with the use of simple percussion instruments such as the tambourine, shaker or maraccas.

Piano lessons can also develop the lateral movement of

both hands together from left to right. The natural tendency is to work out from the centre but finger exercises moving from left to right help to overcome this.

Learning to recognize spatial patterns is dependent upon having a reference point, to which can be related the position of each symbol. Our spatial body position is learnt through the ability to see objects around us, and hear the echoes from them as we move and feel them. We cannot, however, use our body as a reference point to develop visual spatial skills until sufficient body awareness has been developed. 'Musical body' activities and ballet-type movements, together with singing games involving parts of the body all aid this development, as do games such as *This Little Piggy Went to Market* or *Everybody Do This.*

A consistent visual attack is needed before all symbols can be learnt, because a few symbols are identical in every respect, except for their apparent spatial position, which varies according to which eye is dominant in the very small area of central vision of two degrees. A simple experiment demonstrates this: Cover the right eye with the right hand and

119

extend the left hand horizontally in front; with the left hand vertical line up the position of the thumb with a point or object in the background. Leave the left hand in that position and now change the right hand to cover the left eye. Notice how the point or object previously in line with the thumb of the left hand appears to change its position according to which eye is being used.

A failure to establish a stable dominant or reference eye can mean that children are continually varying their direction of attack (for example, looked at from the left outwards this shape is 'd', but from the right it appears as 'b'; see also below. The establishment of a stable dominant or reference eye arises out of much experience in the use of the eyes – a sound is heard and its source sought by the eyes. This process involves constant use of the eye muscles, and so maturity of development is engendered. This means that provided there is no innate weakness or fault the various steps towards mature binocular single vision will be achieved at the usual stages.

Any innate weakness or fault can be identified during the attempts to respond to auditory stimulus, and so ensure that early clinical intervention is provided during the 'critical period' for achieving binocular single vision. Reduction of these attempts, as would occur with children suffering from a minimal hearing loss, not only mean that defects do not mainfest themselves so early, but the 'physical fitness' of the eye muscles do not reach the high standards required for the very demanding literacy skills. Additionally, although 'normal' function is *possible* (and certain tests only demonstrate this), such function is not performed sufficiently often to provide the massive amount of repetition needed for learning. The lack of 'fitness' could also make it difficult to maintain fixation or refixation under dynamic conditions.

Dyslexia

Many eye clinics have noticed how children with squints, who had minor hearing losses, are referred for treatment much later than children with normal hearing. Once binocular single vision and dominance of eye has been established then hand/eye relationships can begin to be realized. When research into dyslexia began it was originally thought that a cross-dominance of hand and eye, that is left eye but right hand dominant, caused children to become dyslexic. More objective research, however, showed that just as many very fine readers as dyslexic children were cross-dominant. My own research shows that does not matter whether dominance is crossed or uncrossed as long as the relationship is stable. Dyslexia is found in children changing from one hand to the other who demonstrate a lack of a stable hand/eye relationship.

The practices in some orthoptic clinics of teaching the child to alternate the fixing eye to preserve binocularity by preventing any degree of amblyopia is, in my opinion, promoting the dyslexic's confusion. In fact, equally acute vision in both eyes must be quite a handicap in establishing a reference eye. Perhaps that is why Valerie Rayner-Smith (1974) and Valerie Spooner (1978) have both remarked upon the lack of dyslexia among those children with manifest squints. It seems that the unequal input aids the development of a reference eye.

I found (in 1960) that occluding the left eye in cases where there appeared to be no established hand/eye relationship, brought immediate relief from confusion during close work. More recently, Sue Fowler has experimented with 30 dyslexic children, giving them for all reading and close work spectacles in which the left lens had been occluded with opaque tape. She found that the reading ages of these children improved by 2.24 months per month of occlusion as against 0.69 month of improvement shown by the non-occluded children. She did, of course, carry out regular checks of visual acuity and convergence training, and reports no drop in vision among the children who were in the experimental group. I have found this to be an essential part of the treatment of dyslexic children who have failed to establish hand/eye references. The Dunlop reference eye test was used to screen those children thought to be suitable for occlusion. The test was found by both Sue Fowler and myself to indicate accurately whether stable relationships had been established or not, but it did not consistently in-idicate which eye was likely to become established as the dominant or preferred eye.

During occlusion, tracing patterns, joining dots and col-ouring shapes can hasten the establishment of the reference eye and the stable hand/eye relationships. Once the child can see the symbols consistently positioned in space, they can be learnt provided sufficient experience is available. Remember that as the same defects which caused the reversals have also caused left and right confusion; remedial activities should also cater for this.

Remedial activities

A ballet movement called *plié* performed in first position, can provide some of the much needed experience in differen-tiating between 'd' and 'b'; this is, of course, subject to the establishment of a preferred eye which makes it possible for the image of the symbol to be consistently positioned on the retina. Explain to the child that when standing with heels together and toes pointed sideways as far as is possible, in preparation for *pliés,* the left foot turned outwards is making the letter 'd' and the right foot, also turned outwards, makes the letter 'b'. Dance instructions can be given on either the 'd' or the 'b' foot; these can move sideways and tap the floor to the music to form reinforcing dance patterns, such as three 'ds' and back to the middle followed by three 'bs' and back to the middle. This can be helped by performing these in front of the mirror.

Action songs such as *I'm a Little Teapot* can be sung and acted in front of the mirror to also reinforce this learning, first with the left arm making the handle shape and the right arm straight up to form the letter 'd'. When singing the letter 'd' the child leans over to the right.

A similar activity can be carried out with the letter 'b' using the right arm to make the handle shape and the left arm to stretch up. Other action songs such as *Left to the Window* also help.

Tap dancing helps develop even greater definition of body

awareness particularly for the short-sighted child, although he rarely reveals serious reading problems other than those obviously associated with his own limited degree of visual acuity.

The move away from the use of lined paper for written exercises overlooks the very important fact, that children need a consistent reference point to produce spatially organized symbols in a consistent manner. Only after there is sufficient experience in this production can the kinaesthetic memory aid the motor system in its reproduction of kinaesthetic sensations by monitoring processes. This monitoring requires not only kinaesthetic memory, but consistent ocular behaviour and motor coordination and control. Kohler, Gregory and others have shown how important touch is to vision. Subjects wearing 'reversing' spectacles found that when touching objects the objects appeared to revert to their normal position in space. A feeling for the outline of shapes can be used to help train the eyes to follow the profile of such shapes; this can also help with the letters 'b' 'd' 'p' and 'q', which present problems, but it is essential, however, to ensure that other information is also available to help place the symbol in its correct spatial position. After all, it is the problem of correct spatial position involving left-to-right eye movement that presents difficulty in bringing the correct image onto the retina. However, if material such as sandpaper with one side smooth and the other corrugated or rough, is used for cutout letters the child can feel the correct face to be presented.

Gregory also points out that objects appeared to be normal when the reversed appearance was physically wrong. This is possibly why a number of dyslexics use capital letters to overcome some of their problems, as 'B' does not exist reversed as 'ᗺ', or 'D' as 'ᗡ'. Perhaps any multisensory support given to visual experience is a key factor in the development of suppression, whether for the child who squints, or one developing normal binocular single vision with the establishment of hand and eye preferences. This support would provide the brain with the additional information needed for a choice between two conflicting or overlapping images.

The difficulty in telling the time often found in children

with this kind of spatial problem, can also be helped by the use of such equipment as the Rotascan Clock (Figure 30) which stimulates the appropriate visual experience needed for such learning. The Rotascan clock demonstrates the passage

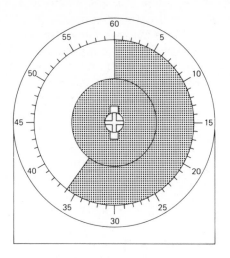

Figure 30 Rotascan Clock

of time and the principles of fractions, decimals, percentages, degrees of a circle and compass points by means of a rotating disc on its face which moves in a clockwise direction. As the disc moves the face gradually 'wipes out', changing colour from white to red.

Feeling the outline of letter shapes with the eyes closed can be used to ensure that they are placed in their correct spatial position, the possibility of the incorrect image being presented for learning will be greatly reduced. The child can only learn what is hears and sees and experiences in other ways. Cutout musical notes, using the same type of material, can be used to aid this training since they produce a similar spatial position as the letters 'b', 'd', 'p' and 'q'; in other words they are all the same except for their spatial position. The lines of the stave add a point of reference.

It must also be remembered that the environment tends to cater only for the right-handed child. Equipment designed for use by the right-handed can, when used by the left-handed, prevent the learning of coordinated movement, in scissors for example just by having the cutting edge on the wrong side. The teacher should always ensure that left-handed children use left-handed scissors.

Conducting is another useful means of providing laterality training as it is a justifiable activity in its own right, so therefore does not keep reminding a child that he is in need of remedial help.

As the duration of a sound affects, very slightly, the pitch sensation received, the child with a slight hearing problem, or one who has missed out of the normal early childhood hearing sensitivity, could have problems in distinguishing between these sounds and so accurately codifying them.

For revising short and long pitched sounds to be played and sung, Baby Humpty Dumpty and Grandma Humpty Dumpty can be used again.

When the full scale can be produced with varying durations then speech sounds can be used, with Baby Humpty Dumpty describing the short sounds and Grandma Humpty Dumpty the long sounds. Initially, they can even be drawn in a similar manner.

a – as in can	a – as in cane
e – as in pet	e – as in pete
i – as in pip	i – as in pipe
o – as in not	o – as in note
u – as in tub	u – as in tube

The next step is to build up the memory span of different pitched sounds and their variations in duration. The teacher can play patterns of pitched sounds on the xylophone starting with any two – C, D, E, F, G, A, B or top C´– listen with eyes closed and then open them and play and sing back from memory.

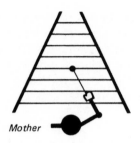

Mother

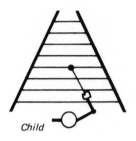

Child

The number of pitched sounds that the child can remember should be increased gradually, each of them lasting a short time.

Auditory training using hearing aids

In my experience I have found that children who suffered from otitis media (inflammation of the middle ear) in babyhood, which is later largely overcome by treatment and/or growth, are greatly helped by auditory training using binaural hearing aids. In these children pure tone audiometry often detects little or no organic hearing loss and tympanometry only reveals the signs of past problems, that is (a) slightly reduced middle ear pressures; (b) depressed or reversed acoustic reflexes; or (c) 'flabby' tubal function.

My research has revealed, however, that many of these children do not discriminate between sounds having less than 50 c.p.s. differential until approximately 30 dB amplification, and that they have little auditory memory, span or repertoire. The greater impact to sound given by the provision of a binaural hearing aid not only overcomes the problems of auditory inattention, day dreaming and withdrawal, but also encourages the pitch discrimination needed for accurate spelling. When listening skills are developed and the auditory memory has established a repertoire of reference points, the hearing aids can be withdrawn gradually. I would strongly advocate this procedure with all children who show signs of poor auditory discrimination and memory, providing noise intolerance is not a problem.

Binaural amplification is recommended because of the spatial awareness needed for all literacy skills, and also provides for:

(1) better learning of direction, distance and spatial awareness;

(2) better localizing of sound sources; less amplification will be needed to obtain better discrimination.

(3) better speech intelligibility even when there is much ambient noise by providing spatial separation of the sound sources.

Many people have noticed that the most minimal hearing loss makes ambient noise a great problem. As literacy processes are spatial skills it is essential for a child to develop spatial awareness; those most at risk are the ones with the most minimal loss, since those with greater losses soon become monaural. If 'intelligence' is the ability to relate information, then the act of comparison involved in its development is also a spatial skill.

Wearing a hearing aid increases the child's awareness of sound, so the child's attention is attracted to the sound itself. Listening must be a continuous activity so that understanding can develop from the ability to continually and consistently hear, and simultaneously observe, the multisensory experience that accompanies each sound. Without a massive amount of such experience the meaning needed for remembering will not be learnt. By wearing these hearing aids the child can then begin to use short and long speech sounds similar to the short and long pitched sounds, thus building up a memory span.

Listening unaided by visual cues such as lip reading should be encouraged by averting the head or covering the mouth when using speech sounds, starting with two of the following:

(o i) (u i) (a e) (u e) (o e) (i e) (e a)

followed by those short sounds:

(o i a) (a i a) (u e a) (i i e)

Again the number can gradually be increased.

This activity should then be repeated with long pitched sounds and then long speech sounds, with eventually a mixture of long and short sounds. Every variation in the spelling of each sound should be introduced, and this is probably best handled in the form of a guessing game. The beginning and ending of words can be missed by children who have a mild hearing loss, as it is often the greater impact of the longer sounds which attracts attention. Playing and singing long and short sounds on each step of the ladder can help to overcome this by training the child to listen more carefully to the beginnings and endings of phrases.

Occasionally a child will pick up the initial sound but not the long vowel sound. Remember also, that consonants should be practised both before and after vowels because of the difference in approach affecting the pitch changes; for example practice both:

b,a   *ba*   as in *bag*
a,b   *ab*   as in gab

remembering that the child will be helped in these activities by the use of binaural hearing aids.

When single words can be reproduced correctly, then proceed to two and three words and so on; do not, however, introduce meaningful sentences or part-sentences until five unassociated words are remembered, because less listening is needed and more guesswork is possible when using meaningful sentences.

Playing with plastic letters can also help develop attention to each sound and so discourage the habit of guessing, which children with this problem so often have. The teacher can try putting the letters into nonsense patterns and ask the child to make sounds such as d, b, p, t, k, and then join them as if they made a word.

Rhythmogrammes

Drawing rhythmogrammes encourages accurate learning. The child listens to a short piece of music and then draws accordingly: *short sounds* are indicated by short lines or dots; *long sounds* are indicated by long lines; *soft sounds* are indicated by thin lines; *loud sounds* are indicated by thick lines.

After drawing rhythmogrammes, when attention to differences in duration are being accurately recognized and remembered, a similar activity using sentences can be developed, for example: I went for a walk. This can be reinforced by movement such as: step, step, run, run, step. Then smaller movements such as in clapping the rhythm: slow, slow, quick, quick, slow.

This can then lead to a form of dance music such as the foxtrot. Following a dancing session many sentences can be devised suitable for rhythm which the child can make up, practise dancing and singing, write and then finally read. For reasons explained above it is important to move from (1) recognizing each unit of the sentence, to (2) gross movement experience of the whole rhythmic pattern, followed by (3) finer experience, (4) much practice of the rhythmic patterns, and finally (5) reading the sentences rhythmically.

Rhythm has its origins in body function, and so can dominate the situation and distract the child's attention from other more sensitive sensory information. However, if rhythm is used too early it can impede the development of pitch memory and discrimination. If it is approached in the manner described above it will ensure that rhythm is used to aid fluency and expression, without preventing attention to the auditory components of language. In some cases 'disco'-type music may provide a stronger, more clearly defined, beat and a greater variety of movement to aid the child whose coordination and spatial learning are severely impaired.

When one coordinated movement has been achieved, then aim for making two continuous, coordinated movements, and then gradually increase the number. Constantly repeating dance patterns is basically sequential training at its best. All sentence patterns can be performed as a dance, and singing them while making the movements enhances learning.

The Benesh notation

Simple dance notation also encourages listening, motor control and coordination. The Benesh notation is based on the music stave and is particularly good for quite small children. It has even been used very successfully in helping spastic children to improve their movement control. This makes sense when one considers how just the act of definition (writing something down) helps to regularize thoughts and so remember them.

In the Benesh notation details of postures and movements are visual; simple marks on a matrix (the five-line stave as used for music) give a clear visual analysis of the human body, the lines intersecting it at shoulder, waist and knees. The person whose movements are to be recorded is imagined as being seen from behind, standing against the five-line stave as if this were painted on a wall. The positions occupied by the hands and feet are marked with dashes, indicating that they lie in the plane of the 'wall'.

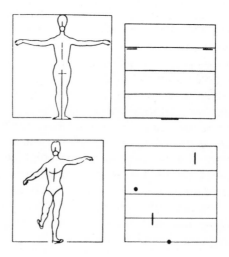

If the limb extends away from the 'wall' other signs are used, vertical strokes indicating positions in front of the 'wall', dots indicating positions behind the 'wall'. These mark the projections of these positions onto the plane of the 'wall'.

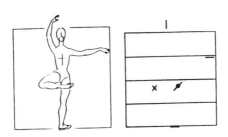

If the limbs are bent, three further signs (derived from the above signs) are used to mark the positions of the elbows or the knees. The basic alphabet, consisting of these six signs only, can record in a precise and completely visual way any position of the limbs.

	Hands or Feet	Elbows or Knees (limbs bent)
Level with the body	—	+
In front of the body	!	+
Behind the body	•	X

Rhythmic shorthand

Rhythmic shorthand (Figure 31) can be used to help develop an awareness of stress pattern in language. Once the basic idea of how the shorthand signs match the notation of duration is understood, it can then be used for both musical and language phrases. Soon a child can be translating the rhythmic shorthand into movement patterns which he can perform imaginatively.

As fluent reading involves rhythm, it has led to the development of various schemes to encourage rhythmic

♩ = l

♩ = h

♩. = m

○ = mn

The	cat	sat	on	the	mat
l	m	l	m	l	h

Figure 31 Simple rhythmic shorthand

reading. Let me, however, repeat my earlier words of warning. The dominance of rhythm, probably arising out of the strength of original learning even prior to birth, could detract from the accuracy of learning individual sensory experiences, but once this learning has taken place then rhythmic work to encourage fluency should be used. At this stage it should also be remembered that rhythm, aided by hearing the resultant sound, involves the ability to feel vibrations. Movement is, therefore, an important activity in developing the rhythmic awareness involved in spatial learning. Any activity which increases the ability to experience the vibration of movement should aid this learning, and the trampoline is a most valuable item of equipment for this. The song *Jack in the Box,* by E. Mellor, is very suitable for this trampoline activity.

Singing games and activities

Rhythmic patterns of movement can be performed to aid the development of memory span while increasing the self-confidence produced by free movements of the body in space. Simple and short patterns such as: two jumps, one turn to the left, sit down and jump up can gradually develop into more complex exercises; chanting the words to the movement will also help. It can also become a 'fun' activity to help develop the awareness of left and right as well as extending the meaningful vocabulary.

It is frequently noticed that children need to concentrate totally during these movement sessions, ignoring all other stimuli. Recently acquired learning with the more severely handicapped children may also appear to be lost when followed by movement, which I suspect is the consequence of restricted neural plasticity. It is only when this particular form of learning is repeated daily for many months, possibly a year, that this loss no longer occurs. When this apparent loss of learning is noticed a number of remedial workers have ceased using movement activities as a form of remediation. In my opinion this should be continued even more energetically, as I believe that this is an encouraging sign in those particular children.

The words of any activity can be set to music for the child to sing while it carriers out the activity.

| Soh | Doh-oh | Doh | Me-e | Me | Soh-oh |

Singing games can be used to introduce intonation patterns. Acting out the old favourite *Ring-a-Ring-a-Roses* can either indicate the end of an activity, or the beginning.

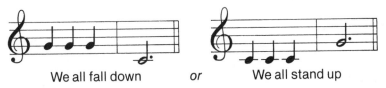

We all fall down   *or*   We all stand up

Making games out of counting the contents of a box, involving the use of the higher note until the last object is counted, are useful. In this game one child sings a high note when he removes each object from the box; on removal of the last object he sings a low note. The other children must recognize whether the object called is the last one to be removed from the box or not, by the pitch of the voice of the child removing the objects from the box. For example if four objects are in the box then the child removing the objects from the box will sing.

One   two   three   four

If, however, the counting is going to continue then the pause is on the higher note.

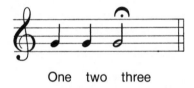

One   two   three

Other intonation patterns can be developed to increase the meaning of language.

The pitch of the final word can change the meaning of a sentence; a high pitch ending brings hope or query whereas the low pitch ending is one of finality.

It is too late?

It is too late!

Falling to a low note at the end of a sentence is used for statements of fact, orders, specific queries and any situation requiring a sense of finality.

It was very cold

Rising to a higher note is used for questions or doubtful remarks, and brings a sense of incompletion or doubt.

Shall I go out?

Singing short sentences and changing the pitch of the final note to alter the meaning can be another activity, and the recognition of musical punctuation yet another. When the meaning and the purpose of the 'full stop' and 'comma' have been explained they can then be taught in their musical form, as rests or 'cadences'. Children can be taught to sit down when hearing a 'full stop' or to stop moving, but remain standing and be ready for more movement when hearing the 'comma' cadence. These can be added to musical games such as 'statues' or 'musical bumps', described above.

Language activities

Each activity should be thought of as a language activity, as after all the repertoire of memorized, meaningful complex sounds organized into spatial patterns that forms the basis of literacy is only a system of notation. Notation has been

135

described by Susan Langer as a means of providing an objective record, a common denominator for thinking and communication, independent of any theory, style or technique. In other words it becomes a means of defining, organizing and learning all previous experiences.

A logical approach based on the ability to learn through the hearing system requires a controlled vocabulary with opportunities for massive repetition of each word once it has been analysed and identified. Every subject in the school curriculum should be approached in this way and not just reading sessions. Remember also how an inability to handle literacy skills tends to prevent the development of interest. To overcome this problem one must *always* begin with a practical and interesting activity, and then the child can record or codify details of the activity in the form of a log book. It is unwise to turn to reading books which have to be decodified, until the child has sufficient experience in codifying the vocabulary in use.

Reading is really a form of testing whether sufficient codifying has taken place. We do not try to test the efficiency of any other skill, without any restriction as to the range of the test, until we have given sufficient opportunity to develop the specific range of that particular skill. Remember, also, that children who have suffered from variations in sensory information arising from quite minor, variable hearing or visual conditions will have very little self-confidence because they have learnt that they cannot trust their own judgement. Much of the material used for the teaching of English as a second language is very useful for these children as the problems are very similar. Science lessons can also be used to improve self-confidence by demonstrating the nature of sound, hearing, light and vision, leading to simple analysis of what is learnt through hearing and vision; the child's own difficulties can be related to this learning process. In this way the children gradually realize that their problems are clinical and unrelated to laziness, stupidity or naughtiness.

Using lessons as an extension of musical learning

The awareness of differences in sound can gradually develop, in conjunction with suitable practical activites. Nature study can become an extension of pitch and tonal discrimination through tape recordings of bird songs and animal sounds, which can then be drawn and described through a controlled vocabulary in a log book. Details about the animals and birds can be collected by the children and suitable reference material, again with a controlled vocabulary, prepared for all the children to use. If each group of children studies a different bird or animal on behalf of the other groups, motivation to codify and so record written details can be developed.

Social studies and creative writing can develop from the attentive listening to recorded environmental sounds – homemade recordings prepared by the children during previous visits to places of interest. Children should be encouraged to prepare 'sound' stories for others to listen, accompanying this with a written report. As mentioned above portable tape recorders are a most valuable teaching aid, and visits to the airport, railway station, shipping port, shopping centre, busy road, bus station, factory, restaurant, zoo etc. provide many interesting sounds. Children should be encouraged to seek out the musical pitch of the sounds by trying to match them with a musical note, all of which aids discrimination. To illustrate a story or play sound effects on musical instruments can also be used.

In history lessons historical events can be transformed into plays illustrated with plenty of homemade sound effects, but keeping within the programme of controlled vocabulary. Studying recordings of early instruments and music both aid auditory discrimination and extend knowledge. Making a model museum can provide more material for the log book. Professional dramatized recordings can also be used to extend the vocabulary range, provide new ideas and enrich learning.

In geography traditional music from around the world can be further introduced by dances which provide opportunities for greater coordination and spatial learning. Human

F

geography can be approached by the songs of the various in-dustries such as the Welsh miners, the cotton spinners and so on: visits to the areas covered, if possible, can produce more material for written work.

For secondary school children cookery lessons can become an extension of the modelling experience needed in developing hand/eye relationships. Craft lessons can produce homemade musical instruments for tuning and playing. Technical drawing can be an extension of orthoptic training because of the greater control and detail required. Modern languages provide further opportunities for sound discrimina-tion. Patterns of digits can be danced to music, jumped to on a trampoline, acted to through movement or played on a xylophone. In short, every subject in the primary or secondary school's normal curriculum can be approached in this manner to assist the development of the spatially organized language components.

Using musical instruments in helping speech problems

Certain speech problems or defects can be helped by work with a musical instrument. A speech sound weak in sound level can be given greater power when transferred to a musical note on a wind instrument.

The difference between 'f' and 'th', frequently a great pro-blem, can be demonstrated and *heard* on the flute.
'T' and 'D' develops when tongued separately on the trumpet.

Playing pitched sounds on a variety of instruments can help to build up greater vowel discrimination.

One of the problems in teaching hard-of-hearing children to produce consonants correctly is the attempt to teach an in-terruption of a continuous sound as if it were a continuing sound (rather like during the days of the Second World War when we talked about hearing a 'doodlebug' stop!) Producing a variety of continuing sounds on wind instruments according to the consonants used gives the child a sound which is fre-quently loud enough to be heard and so copied, and eventually the kinaesthetic sensation of making that sound can be copied without the use of the instrument. A recorder can also provide simple orthoptic training for the child as he checks the position of his fingers on the instrument and then looks at the notation on the board in the distance.

However, a homemade bamboo pipe is even better as the shape of the mouthpiece can be varied to cope with individual problems (such as for the spastic child who may need a thicker mouthpiece).

Singing lessons are yet another way of improving language skills. The relaxation of the vocal organs (essential otherwise singing becomes physiologicaly impossible) is often all that is needed to overcome stuttering. The precious few extra decibels of hearing provided in the singing of a sound not only help the learning of the sound, but often also appear to increase the speed of feedback to the brain; the soft singing of vowel sounds therefore leads to the development of greater discriminination. As singing of necessity leads to greater intake of oxygen this in turn increases the sense of wellbeing, stimulates learning and improves muscle tone.

It is important to realize how vital is the improvement of self-image for children who have experienced failure. Additionally, it must not be forgotten that unreliable sensory systems create uncertainty and therefore destroy self-confidence; this must be overcome together with the problems that will arise from the prevention of the continuous collection of information, normally experienced through a correctly functioning sensory system. For instance, the dyslexic child's collection of interesting information to handle and process, and from which grows the snowball effect necessary for the development of an enquiring mind, is often hampered even more than the child who is severely deaf or blind but who is receiving special teaching. Practical activities, unrestricted by literacy problems, must therefore take place throughout the remediation programmes, ensuring that by the time the child is beginning to become literate he has something of interest to read or write about.

The above ideas are just a few ways in which musical activities can be used for preparing children to become fully literate and functioning members of the community. With a little ingenuity many more ways can and must be developed.

Pitch training

The importance of pitch training in developing literacy skills and intelligence is demonstrated in the following research projects and papers.

Desmond Sergeant and Gillian Thatcher (1973) give details of the low correlation between general intellectual abilities and musical abilities shown by many researchers such as Hollingworth, Cox, etc. They quote Cleak's observation that empirically there appears to be a dichotomy between experience in general classroom situations, and in research. In my opinion, the apparent dichotomy disappears when one specifies the component skills of musical abilities, as however varied the list may be it will always include both sensitivity of intonation and pitch memory.

The learning of pitch at the prepuberty stage is not affected by intelligence, and sensitivity of intonation can even be greater among the lower ability group because, as shown in the Suffolk experiment, the threshold of boredom is reached much more slowly so meaningful pitch training can go on for a longer period. The work of Suzuki also suggests that much of what is described as musical feeling and interpretation is the result of auditory conditioning to establish interpretative patterns. Other aspects of musical ability make varying cognitive demands on the subject, but these could be assisted by the learnt degree of sensitivity for intonation and absolute pitch. This in my opinion, could explain the lack of correlation between 'intellectual variables and musical tests'.

Imhofer of the Zurich University Medical School, points out the 'unusually narrow vocal range' of the subnormal child, but also remarks that 'musical receptivity is often better developed in the mentally retarded'. In a study of 30 children (8 to 9 years) with IQ assessments of below 100 (Schonell Tests) at a residential special school, and compared with 30 children with IQs of over 120 of the same group in the Junior Department of a Direct Grant School, I made the following observations.

The lower ability group needed a far greater amount of drilling in the association of either notation or tonic solfa with pitch than the higher ability group. The lower ability group received daily training in this association, 5 days a week for 20 minutes a day, and took 3 weeks to attain the standard of notation recognition achieved by the higher ability group in two sessions of 40 minutes each.

The higher ability group were able to respond more quickly to notation but showed less accurate intonation than the lower ability group. The lower ability group also showed greater accuracy of pitch memory than the higher group when tested orally, but often made mistakes when translating the oral work into written work using traditional notation. A greater exactness of pitch was shown by the lower ability group and better tone quality when singing, due, I believe, to copying more exactly the sample given. It is interesting to note in the results of Suffolk-based research over a period of nearly 8 years, on the implications of audio-comparative language programmes and concept glyphs to the teaching of retarded and mentally subnormal children, the reference to certain aspects of language which requires constant repetition, possibly a minimum of 30 to 40 times. This proved to be more acceptable to less intelligent children since the threshold of boredom was reached more slowly. Also, providing hearing aids to a group of subnormal children with no recorded hearing loss improved all-round performance. Pitch training produced the same results, as did the auditory training given to the hearing-impaired in that it developed the ability to listen.

I then carried out an experiment in a school to measure the effects of auditory presentation and training. A piece of prose was selected for study by a group of 20 children of 10 +, IQ range 90−100 (Schonell Tests A and B), who had received pitch training together as a class in daily sessions of 20 minutes for 6 months. Ten children (Group A) went into one room and were given a sample of prose to study, in silence, for

10 minutes (Schonell, 1962). They were not allowed to write anything down.

The other ten children (Group B) were then each given a copy of the same test but were seated in listening booths, where tape-recorded samples of the test were available. Each child wore headphones and listened to the recorded sample while following his or her printed copy of the test. This was repeated over and over again for 10 minutes. Both groups were then given a question paper to test retention.

A stongly significant difference was found between the mean scores when using the visual method and the audio-visual method, both before and after pitch training.

The daily sessions of pitch learning were carried out in the following manner:

(1) Soundproof cubicles were available for individual use whenever required, complete with tape-recorders and head-phones.

(2) Tape-recorded texts of all set works were provided so that they could be presented, slightly amplified and at the meatus, by the use of headphones.

(3) Dramatized recordings of set works or topics were provided whenever possible.

(4) Five sets of 'B and H Language Master' equipment was provided for work requiring a great deal of audio-visual repetition.

In 1963 twelve of these youngsters took the O level GCE examination. The subjects covered were Geography, English Language, English Literature (syllabus B), Mathematics (syllabus B), German, Music and General Science. Those candidates taking Geography, English Language, the optional Spoken English examination, English Literature (syllabus B) and German, had all received extensive audio-visual training in the soundproof booths in addition to the usual class work. In each of these subjects the passes obtained were between 85% and 100%.

While it must be remembered that successes recorded in

percentages with small groups can appear exaggerated, a comparison with the 1963 O level examination results as shown in Table 3 is most interesting.

	Comprehensive school (mixed ability)	Secondary modern school IQ 85–100	Technical school IQ 112–120	Unrecognized independent school (mixed ability); often unqualified teachers	Grammar school IQ 120 +
Geography	62.6	49.1	49.2	46.0	67.7
English Language	39.6	32.5	43.0	27.8	67.5
German	32.5	11.4	21.3	15.1	53.4
English Literature (B)	36.1	32.9	43.5	33.8	55.6
Music	61.5	40.0	44.4	21.1	67.0

Table 3 GCE examination (ordinary level) passes 1963 – expressed as a percentage

These examination results were sufficiently dramatic to resut in a major Local Education Authority instructing their psychologist to reassess the pupils as these results appeared to contradict IQ assessments; the latter, however, were found not to be error:

Considering the vast range of possible multisensory consequences of early childhood hearing disorders that continue long after the original defect has been overcome or outgrown leads us to the child who is intelligent but underachieving in language skills. A study of the nature of the deprivation existing during such disorders helps to identify the form of treatment and remediation needed. This is a combination of music and medicine.

The medical side is brought in, because although the hearing defect is often no longer sufficiently present to be identified by the routine audiometric test standardized on adults, help is often needed to bridge the gap between childhood and adult sensitivity to sound remembering that a memory of previously learnt sounds is needed to identify what is later heard. Similarly, the consequences of the reduced impact of sound may, to mention but one factor, include a failure to establish a stable reference eye and powers of convergence to cope with skills involving dynamic lateral movement; this could be treated by an orthoptist.

Music education is an ongoing process concerned with developing the child's multisensory awareness and response to the vast range of sounds, and teaching how to discriminate between such variations. It is therefore concerned with both diagnosis and remediation of problems, evoking and supporting normal development, and could be described as the physiology and psychology of hearing.

Music is thus truly the source of all learning.

Bibliography

Abel-Struth, Sigrid (1974). *The Problem of Socialization by Learning Music in Early Childhood,* ISME Seminar

Abramowitz, Arnold (1971). Devising a development test of auditory perception, problems and prospects, *J. S. African Speech and Hearing Assoc.,* **Vol. 18**

Abramowitz, Arnold. *The Problems and Prospects of Devising a Development Test of Aural Perception,* Psychology Department, University of Cape Town

Agnew, Marie (1922). A comparison of auditory images of musicians, psychologists and children, *Psychol. Monogr.,* **Vol. 31,** 268–78.

Agnew, Marie (1922). The auditory images of great composers, *Psychol. Mongr.,* **Vol. 31,** 279–87

Alvin, J. (1965). *Music for the Handicapped Child.* Oxford University Press

Anderson, T. (1939). Variations in the normal range of childrens voices, variation in the range of tone audition, variation in pitch discrimination. Unpublished PhD thesis, Edinburgh University

Anson and Donaldson, *Surgical Anatomy of the Temporal Bone and Ear, 2nd Ed.* Saunders

Apel, Willi. *Notation of Polyphonic Music,* 900–1600

Bachem, A. (1937). Various types of absolute pitch. *J. Acoust. Soc. Amer.,* **9,** 146–151

Bachem, A. (1940). The genesis of absolute pitch, *J. Acoust. Soc. Amer.,* **11,** 434–439

Bachem, A. (1948). Note on Neu's review of the literature on absolute pitch, *Psychol.,* **B 45,** 161–162

Bachem, A. (1954). Time factors in relative and absolute pitch determination, *J. Acoust. Soc. Amer.,* **26.5,** 751−53

Bagenal, Hope. *Practical Acoustics,* Methuen

Baggaley, J. P. (1973). *Colour and Musical Pitch,* Audio-visual Aids, Unit, University of Liverpool

Baines, A. (1961). *Musical Instruments through the Ages,* Pelican

Baird, J. W. (1917), *Memory for Absolute Pitch; Studies in Psychology, Titchener Commemorative Volume,* pp. 43−78, Worcester: Wilson

Bannatye, Alexander (1971). *Language, Reading and Learning Disabilities,* Springfield, Ill.: C. C. Thomas

Bannister, R. (1975). *Brain's Clinical Neurology.*

Bartholomew, W. T. (1916). *Acoustics of Music,* Prentice Hall

Bartle, Graham A. R. (1974). *Comparative Music Education − A Vital Discipline in Its Infancy,* ISME Seminar

Bean, Kenneth L. (1938). An experimental approach to the reading of music, *Psychol. Monogr.,* **Vol. 50,** No. 6, 80

Beardwood, C. J. (1973). Audiogenic stimulation of urinary gonadotrophin output in man, *S. African Med. J.,* **June 1973,** 47

Beck, E. W. *Anatomy of the Human Ear*

Békésy, G. von and Rosenblith, W. A. (1951). The mechanical properties of the ear. In Stevens, S. S. (ed.) *Handbook of Experimental Psychology.* New York: Wiley

Békésy G. von (1955). Human skin perception of travelling waves similar to those on the cochlea. *J. Acoust. Soc. Amer.,* **27,** 830−41

Békésy G. von (1963). Three experiments concerned with pitch perception; *J. Acoust. Soc. Amer.,* **35.4,** 602−606

Benesh, Rudolf and Benesh Joan (1969). *An Introduction to Benesh Movement Notation.* A. C. Black

Bentley, Arnold (1966). *Musical Ability in Children.* Harrap

Bienstock, Sylvia F. (1942). A review of recent studies on musical aptitude. *J. Ed. Psychol.,* **33,** 427−442

Blakeslee, B. (1963). *The Limb Deficient Child.* University of California Press

Blacking, J. (1970). Tonal organisation in Venda music. *J.*

Soc. Ethnomusicol.

Blacking, John (1967). *Musical Expeditions of the Venda; African Music 3 (i),* Witwatersrand University Press

Blacking, John. *Towards a Theory of Musical Competence.* Witwatersrand University Press

Blind, E. E. (1938). An experiment with monotones. *Mus. Educ.,* **J. 24,** 37–39

Boggs, C. P. (1907). Studies in absolute pitch. *Amer. J. Psychol.,* **18,** 194–205

Brammer, (1951). Sensory cues in pitch judgement. *J. Exper. Psychol.,* **41,** 336–40

Brandt, John F. and Hollien, Harry (1967). Underwater Hearing thresholds in man; *J. Acoust. Soc.Amer.,* **Vol. 42.** No. 5

Brandt, John F. and Hollien, Harry (1968). Underwater speech reception thresholds and discrimination, *J. Auditory Res.,* **8,** 71–80

Brandt, John F. and Hollien, Harry (1969). Underwater Hearing thresholds in man as a function of water depth, *J. Acoust. Soc. Amer.,* **Vol. 46,** No. 4

Brehmar, F. (1925). In Teplov, B. M., *Psychologie des Aptitudes Musicales.* Presses Universitaires de France (1966).

Brehmer, F. (1925). *Melodieauffassuno und Melodische; Bebang des Kindes.*

Bridges, Doreen (1974). *Development of the Australian Test for Advanced Music Studies,* ISME Seminar

Brink, van den, G. (1970). *Experiments on Binaural Diplacusis and Tone Perception.*

Broadbent, D. E. (1962). *Attention and the Perception of Speech,* Freeman

Brown, Roger (1968). *Words and Things,* Free Press

Bruford, Rose (1948). *Speech and Drama,* Methuen

Bruner, J. S. (1963). *The Process of Education,* Vintage Press

Bullock, (1975). Report – March 1975; London: HMSO

Bunch, (1943). *Clinical Audiometry,* London: Henry Kimpton

Burns, W. (1968). *Noise and Man,* Murrays

Byrd, Audrey S. (1974). *Music and Dyslexia,* University of Cape Town

Byrd, Audrey S. (1972). *A Survey of the Literature on the Language Acquisition of the Child,* College of Education, Middleton St George UK

Cady, H. L. (1976). *Fundamental Problems in the Improvement of Music Education,* ISME Conference, Montreux

Carlsen, James C. (1976). *University of Washington, USA, Cross-Cultural Influences on Expectancy in Music,* ISME Conference, Montreux

Carmichael, L. (1954). The onset and early development of behaviour. In *Manual of Child Psychology,* New York: Wiley

Carpenter, M. B. (1964). *Ascending vestibular projections and conjugate horizontal eye movements*

Carpenter, R. H. S. (1977). *Movements of the Eyes*

Cattell, W. (1967). *Objective Personality and Motivation Tests,* University of Illinois Press

Cashell and Durran (1974). *Handbook of Orthoptic Principles.*

Causley, Marguerite (1967). *A Language for Movement.*

Chapman, A. (1960). *Speech Training and Practice,* Oliver and Boyd

Choksy, Lois. *The Kodaly Method,* Prentice Hall

Churchley, Frank (1974). *Some Recent Canadian Developments in Research in the Study of Music,* ISME Seminar

Clark, Margaret (1957). *Left Handedness,* University of London Press

Corner, G. W. (1944). *Ourselves Unborn; an Embryologist's Essay on Man,* New Haven: Yale University Press

Courtney, Richard (1965). *Teaching Drama,* Unwin Brothers Limited

Critchley, McDonald (1977). *Music and the Brain.*

Crook, W. G. (1975). *Can your Child Read? Is he hyperactive?*

Crystal, David (1972). *Non-Segmental Phonology in Language Acquisition; A Review of the Issues,* Reading University, UK

Curtis, Holbrook. *Voice Building and Tone Placing,* Appleton Company

Curtis, S. J. (1965). *Philosophy of Education,* University Tutorial Press

Curwen, J. (1958). *How to Read and Understand Music,* University of London Press

Cykler, E. A. (1974). *Comparative Music Education,* ISME Seminar

Davies, J. B. (1971). *New Tests of Music Aptitude. Br. J. Psychol.,* **62.4.** 557—65

Davis, Hallowell (1960). *Hearing and Deafness,* Holt, Rinehart and Winston

Davson, H. (1972). *Physiology of the Eye,* Churchill Livingstone

Delaney, M. E., Whittle, L. S. and Knox, E. C. (1966). A note on the use of self recording audiometry with children. *J. Laryngol.,* **Vol. 80**

Denenberd, V. H. *Early Experience and Emotional Development,* Freeman and Co.

Denes, P. B. and Mathews, M. V. (1968). *Computer Models for Speech and Music Appreciation,* Joint Computer Conference

Denes, P. B. and Pinsin, E. N. (1967). *The Speech Chain,* Bell Telephone Laboratories

Ditchburn, R. W. *Eye Movements and Visual Perception.*

Dobbs, J. (1972). *The Slow Learner,* Oxford University Press

Drake, Raleigh M. (1954). *Drake Musical Aptitude Tests.*

Dunlop, P. (1974). *New Concepts of Visual Laterality in Relation to Dyslexia.*

Dunlop, P. (1976). *The Changing Role of Orthoptics in Dyslexia.*

Dunlop, P. *A New Orthoptic Technique in Learning Disability.*

Dunlop, P. (1977). *Orthoptics in Dyslexia.*

Du Preez, Peter (1972). *Tone Groups, Information and Language Acquisition,* University of Cape Town

Dutoit, C. L. (1976). *Eurhythmics, Its Value and Relevance,* Geneva: Pub. Institut Jaques-Dalcroze

Dykema, Peter W. (1948). Some fundamental questions about music reading. *Mus. Educ. J.,* **35,** 24—26

Emmett, E. R. (1966). *Learning to Philosophize,* Longmans

Encyclopaedia Britannica (1968). *Finding Out about Musical*

Education and Training in Britain, Britannica Extension Service

Encyclopaedia Britannica (1970). *Programmed Learning,* Britannica Extension Service

Encyclopaedia Britannica (1970). *Studying the Brain,* Britannica Extension Service

Fernandez (1955). The effect of oxygen lack on cochlea potentials. *Amer. Otol. Rhinol. Laryngol.*

Fjerdingsgad (1971). *Chemical Transfer of Learned Information,* Amsterdam: North-Holland Publishing Co.

Flavell, J. H. (1970). *Development Psychology of Jean Piaget,* Van Nostrand Reinhold Company

Fletcher, *Speech and Hearing.*

Fridman, Ruth (1944). *Sonorous-Rhythmic Expressions of Babies in Relation to Future Music Ability and Articulated Language,* ISME Seminar

Frisby, J. P. (1979). *Seeing. Illusion, Brain and Mind,* Oxford University Press

Fromer, E. *Voyage through Childhood into the Adult World.*

Fry, D. B. (1964). *The Deaf Child,* Heinemann.

Fry, D. B. (1977). *Man as a Talking Animal,* Cambridge University Press

Funchess, L. V. (1949), Research is needed in musical education, *Phi. Delta Kappan,* **30,** 349−50

Galambos, R. and Davies, H. (1943). The response of single auditory-nerve fibres to acoustic stimulation, *J. Neurophysiol.,* **6,** 39−58

Garder, Clarence E. (1954). Characteristics of outstanding high school musicians, *J. Res. Mus. Educ.,* **Vol. 2,** 11−20

Gardiner, William. *The Music of Nature.*

Gesell, Arnold and Ilg, F. L. (1949). Child development: an introduction to the study of human growth; Harper 403, p. 475,

Gesell, Arnold, Ilg, F. L. and Ames, (1974). *The Child from Five to Ten.*

Gibson, J. J. (1966). *The Senses Considerd as Perceptual Systems,* London: George Allen and Unwin

Gilles, Mary G. (1909). An experimental study of musical

learning, *Arch. Psychol.*, **No. 12,** 71–78, Columbia University

Gordon, A. G. (1976). *Arch. Otolaryngol.*

Gordon, A. G. (1976). *Med. Hypotheses*

Gordon, A. G. (1976). *Develop. Med. Child Neurol.*

Gordon, A. G. (1977). *J. Autism Child. Schizophrenia*

Gordon, A. G. (1977). *J. Otolaryngol.*

Gordon, A. G. (1977). *Med. J. Aust.*

Grodon, A. G. (1977). *Lancet* (by R. W. Hayes and AGG).

Gordon, A. G. (1978). *J. Autism Child. Schizophrenia*

Gordon, A. G, (1978). *Paediatrics*

Gordon, A. G. (1978). *Amer. Heart J.*

Gordon, A. G. (1978). *J. Neurosurg.*

Gordon, A. G. (1979). *Brit. Med. J.*

Gordon, A. G. (1979). *Hearing*

Gordon, A. G. (1979). *Otitis Media in Infancy*

Graves, W. S. (1947). Factors associated with children taking music lessons, including some parent/child relationships, *Ped. Sem.,* **70,** 65–125

Gregory, R. C. (1977). *Eye and the Brain.*

Guberina, Verbo-Tonal Method; Revue de Phonetique Applique, Vol. 3, Tulasiewicz.

Guelke, R. W. and Smith, E. D. (1963). Distribution of information in stop consonants, *Proceedings IEE,* **Vol. 110,** No. 4

Gunild and Keetman, *Orff Schulwerk,* Schott and Co.

Hall, George (1972). *Applied Human Cybernetics,* J. Session.

Harper, W. M. (1971). *Statistics,* Macdonald and Evans

Haskell, S. H. (1977). *The Education of Motor and Neurologically Handicapped Children.*

Hattwick, Melvin S. (1933). The role of pitch level and pitch range in the singing of pre-school, first and second grade school children, *Child Develop,* **4,** 281–291

Hawkins, Eric (1971). Communication and language – the importance of the early years, *Contact,* **October**

Hebb, D. O. (1949). *The Organisation of Behaviour; A Neuropsychological Theory,* New York: Wiley and Sons

Helmholtz, H. L. F. von (1912). *The Sensations of Tone,* London: Longmans

Henkin, R. I. (1955). A factorial study of the components of music, *J. Psychol,* **39,** 161—81

Henning, G. B. (1965), Effect of 'aural harmonics' on frequency discrimination, *J. Acoust. Soc. Amer.,* **37,** 1144

Henry, S. (1947). *Children's Audiograms in Relation to Reading Attainment,* University of North Carolina

Hevner, Kate (1937). The effective value of pitch and tempo in music, *Amer, J. Psychol.,* **49,** 621—630

Hickman, Aubrey (1970). *Experiments with Children Involving Pitch, Rhythm and Timbre; Research in Educ. No. 3,* Manchester University Press

Hoermann, Deanna B. (1974). *Music Education in Early Childhood.*

Hoffer, C. R. (1974). *Study of the Effectiveness of the Curwen—Kodaly Hand Signals,* ISME Seminar

Hollien, Harry (1973). Underwater sound localization in humans, *J. Acoust. Soc. Amer.,* **Vol. 53,** No. 5

Hollien, Harry and Brandt, John F. (1969). Effect of air bubbles in the external auditory meatus on underwater hearing thresholds, *J. Acoust. Soc. Amer.,* **Vol. 46,** No. 2

Hollien, Harry and Feinstein, Stephen (1975). Contribution of the external meatus to auditory sensitivity underwater, *J. Acoust. Soc. Amer.,* **Vol. 57,** No. 6, Communication Sciences Laboratory, University of Florida.

Hollingworth, Leta S. (1926). Musical sensitivity of children who test above 135 IQ, *J. Ed. Psychol.,* **17,** 95—109

Honda, M. *A Programme for Early Development.*

Hughes, A. G. and E. H. (1959). *Learning and Teaching,* Longmans

Hughes, Jo. Ann M. (1955). Fifty-nine case studies on the effect of musical participation on sound development, *Mus. Educ. J.,* **41,** 58—59

Huxley, Renika (1967). *Language, Chimpanzees and Children.*

Hyatt King A. *Four Hundred Years of Music Printing.*

Ingram, T. *Study of the Educational Attainment of Children with Deviant Speech Development,* University of Edinburgh

Irwin, Orvis (1949). *Infant Speech,* Freeman

Isaacs, S. (1956). *The Children We Teach,* University of London Press

Ittelson, W. and Kilpatrick, F. (1951). *Experiments in Perception,* Freeman

Jacobsen, O. Irving (1933). The influence of hearing defects, *Mus. Supervisors J.,* **19,** 24—25

Jacobsen, O. Irving (1942). An analytical study of eye movements in reading, vocal and instrumental music, *J. Musicol.,* **3,** 197

James, Margaret (1972). *The Pipers Guild Handbook,* Pipers Guild

Jeans, James (1938). *Science and Music,* Cambridge University Press

Jersild, Arthur T. (1939). Music. In *Child Development and the Curriculum; 38th Yearbook, Part 1,* NSSE Public Sch. 135—151

Johnson, S. (1969). *Achieving Reading Success,* C.A.L.

Jones, R. L. *Nature of Language,* American Telephone Research Laboratory

Jones, R. O. and Pracey, R. (1971). An investigation of pitch discrimination in the normal and abnormal hearing adult, *J. of Laryngol.*

Joyner, D. R. (1971). *Pitch Discrimination and Tonal Memory and Their Association with Singing and the Larynx,* Unpublished MPhil. thesis, University of Reading

Karlin, J. E. (1942). A factorial study of auditory function, *Psychometrika,* **7,** 251—279

Karlovitch, R. S. (1968). Sensory interaction, perception of loudness during visual stimulation, *J. Acoust. Soc. Amer.,* **44,** 2, 570—575

Kemp, A. E. *A Pilot Study of the Personality Pattern of Creative Music Students,* Sussex University

Kendall, M. G. *Rank Correlation Methods,* London: Griffin

Kern, M. R. (1922). Report on corrective treatment of a group of monotones; *E. Sch. J.,* **23,** 197

Kimura, D. (1961). Cerebral dominance and the perception of verbal stimuli, *Canad. J. Psychol.,* **16,** 18—22

King, H. A. (1939). *Auditory and Visual Characteristics of*

Poor Music Readers, PhD thesis, New York University

Kittle, J. Leslie (1932). Music education and scientific research, *Music Observers J.,* **18,** 37

Knight, (1966). *Modern Introduction to Psychology,* University Tutorial Press

Knight, J. J. (1971). Lecturer in Psycho and Physical Acoustics, Postgraduate Institute of Otology and Laryngology, London

Ladefoged, P. (1962). *Elements of Acoustic Phonetics,* Oliver and Boyd

Ladefoged, P. *Information Conveyed by Vowels.*

Lamb, L. E. and Dunckel, D. C. (1976). *Acoustic Impedance Measurement with Children,* Baltimore, Md: Williams and Wilkins

Langer, S. K. (1953). *Feeling and Form,* Routledge

Langer, S. K. (1960). *Philosophy in a New Key,* Harvard University Press

Lenihan, J. M. A. (1971). The threshold in school children, *J. of Laryngol.*

Larson, William S. (1951). *Bibliography of Research Studies in Music Education,* Music Educators National Conference, 132

Lenneberg (1967). *Biological Foundations of Language,* J. Wiley and Son

Levine, Seymour (1971). Stress and behaviour, *Sci. Amer.,* **January,** No. 1, 26–31

Liberman, A. M. *Some Results of Research on Speech Perception.*

Liess, A. (1966). *Carl Orff.* Calder and Boyars

Ling, D. (1976). *Speech and the Hearing Impaired Child*

Littler, T. S. (1965). *Physics of the Ear,* Pergamon Press

Lloyd, Barbara (1972). *Perception and Cognition,* Penguin

Lovell, K. (1969). *Educational Psychology and Children,* University of London Press

Lumsdaine, A. and Glasser, R. (1961). *Teaching Machines and Programmed Learning,* National Educ. Assoc. USA

Lundin, Robert W. (1949). The development and validation of

a set of musical ability tests, *Psychol. Monogr.,* **Vol. 63,** 305, 20

Luria, A. R. (1973). *The Working Brain.*

Lyle and Wybar, (1977). *Practical Orthoptics in the Treatment of Squint,* Lewis

Mackarness, R. (1976). *Not all in the Mind.*

Mager, R. F. Preparing Educational Objectives.

Marshall, G. M. (1977). *The Eyes and Vision.*

Marteniuk, Ronald G. (1976). *Human Motor Performance,* Holt, Rinehart and Winston

Martin, F. (1953). *The Jaques-Dalcroze Eurhythmics,* Brussels: International Congress for Musical Education

Martin, J. A. M. and Martin, Dorothy (1973). Auditory perception, *Brit. Med. J.,* **2,** 459−461

Martin, M. C. (1974). *Critical Bands in Sensori-Neural Hearing Loss,* London: Royal National Institute for the Deaf

Maurer, Y. (1969). *The Cover Test; A Guide to Its Diagnostic and Prognostic Potential.*

McAllister, Anne H. (1939). *Steps in Speech Training.* University of London Press

McGraw, Myrtle B. (1943). *Neuromuscular Maturation of the Human Infant,* Columbia University

McLeish, John (1950). The validation of seashore's measure of musical talent by factorial methods, *Brit. J. Psychol. Stat.,* **Sect. 3,** 129−140

McLeish, John (1966). *The Factor of Musical Cognition in Wing's and Seashore's Tests,* Music Education Research Papers, No. 2

McLuhan, Marshall (1971). *Understanding Media,* Sphere Books Ltd.

Mee, F. G. (1967). *Sounds,* Heinemann Educational Books Ltd.

Merrill, Terman (1964). *Stanford−Binet Intelligence Scale,* Harrap

Meyer, M. (1899). Is memory of absolute pitch capable of development by training? *Psychol. Rev.,* **6,** 514−516

Michel, Paul (1974). *The Necessity of an Early Development of Musical Talents at Pre-School Age and the Problem of*

Aptitude Diagnosis, ISME Seminar

Miller, Dayton. *The Science of Musical Sounds,* Methuen

Miller, G. A. (1962). *Psychology,* Pelican

Millerson, Gerald (1970). *Technique of T.V. Production,* Focal Press

Millikan and Darley. *Brain Mechanisms Underlying Speech and Langauge.*

Moore, B. C. J. (1972). Frequency difference limens for narrow bands of noise, *J. Aconot. Soc. Amer.*

Moses, P. J. (1959). The vocal expression of emotional disturbance, *Kaiser Foundation Med. Bull.,* **7,** 107–111

Mountcastle, V. B. (1962). *Inter-Hemispheric Relations Cerebral Dominance,* Johns Hopkins Press

Mull, H. K. (1925). The acquisition of absolute pitch, *Amer. J. Psychol.,* **36,** 469–493

Murphy, K. P. and Smyth, C. N. (1962). Response of Foetus to Auditory Stimulation, *Lancet,* **5 May,** 972–973

Mursell, J. L. (1947). Growth gradient in music, *Mus. Educ. J.,* **34,** 18–19

Negus, V. E. (1949). *The Comparative Anatomy and Physiology of the Larynx,* Hafner Publishing Company

Neisser (1966). *Cognitive Psychology,* Meredith Corporation

Neu, D. M. (1947). A critical review of the literature on 'absolute pitch', *Psychol. Brit,* **44,** 249–266

Nicholl, B. (1978). *Perspectives in Coeliac Disease.*

Nordoff, P. and Robbin, Clive (1971). *Therapy and Music for Handicapped Children,* Victor Gollancz

Nye, Robert E. (1953). If you don't use syllables, what do you use? *Music Educ. J.,* **39,** 41–42

Oakes, W. F. (1955). An experimental study of pitch naming and pitch discrimination reactions, *J. Genet. Psychol.,* **86,** 237–259

Oates, J. (1979). *Early Cognitive Development.*

O'Connor, D. J. (1956). *An Introduction to the Philosophy of Education,* Routledge and Kegan Paul

O'Connor, Otto R. (1937). *Span of Vision in Note Reading; 30th Yearbook,* Musical Educ. National Conference pp. 88–93

Ostwald, Peter F. and Peltzman, P. (1974). The cry of the human infant, *Sci. Amer.,* Freeman and Co.

Paget, R. (1963). *Human Speech,* Routledge and Kegan Paul

Pampiglione-Bassi, Emma (1964). *La ritmica integrate di Laura Bassi,* Brescia: La Scuola

Parrish, Carl — *Notation of Mediaeval Music.*

Paynter, John — *Sound and Silence,* Cambridge University Press

Peters, R. S. (1966). *Ethics and Education,* George Allen and Unwin Ltd.

Peters, R. S. (1967). *Concept of Education,* Routledge and Kegan Paul

Peterson, Lloyd (1966). Short-Term Memory, Freeman and Co.

Petran, L. A (1932). An experimental study of pitch recognition, *Psychol. Monogr.,* **193,** XL11, No. 6

Pflederer-Zimmerman, Marilyn (1974). *Conservation in Musical Experience,* ISME Seminar

Polish Government Report (1970). *Program Wychowania Muzycznnego W. Klasach I – II/Nauczanie Poczatkowe/,* ISME Seminar

Polish Government Report (1970). *Program Wychowania Muzycznnego W. Klasach III – V/Nauczanie Systematyczne/,* ISME Seminar

Pollack, D. (1975). *Educational Audiology for the Limited Hearing Infant.*

Porte, D. (1976). *Towards a Better Understanding of the Jaques-Dalcroze Method.*

Prescott, J. W., Read, M. S. and Cousin, D. B. 'Brain Function and Malnutrition'.

Punt, Norman (1967). *The Singers' and Actors' Throat,* Heinemann Medical Books

Rands, Bernard — *Sound Patterns,* Universal Edition

Ray, B. (1975). Requirements and problems of hearing underwater, *Brit. Soc. of Audiol. Soc. for Underwater Technol.*

Rayner-Smith, V. (1974). *Ocular Dominance/Binocular Vision.*

Reed, G. F. (1964). *The Association of Auditory High Frequency Weakness with Verbal and Written Com-*

prehension and Expression, University of Durham

Ravesz, G. (1953). *Introduction to the Psychology of Music,* London: Longman Green

Richardson, E. G. (1929). *The Acoustics of Orchestral Instruments and the Organ,* E. Arnold and Co.

Riker, B. L. (1946). The ability to judge pitch, *J. Exper. Psychol.,* **36,** 331−346

Risset, Jean-Claude and Mathews, Max V. (1969). Analysis of musical instrument tones, *Phy. Today,* **Vol. 22,** No. 2

Ritchie, Russell W. (1975). *Explaining the Brain,* Oxford University Press

Rodda, Michael (1967). *Noise and Security,* Oliver and Boyd

Roederer, J. G. (1973). *Introduction to the Physics and Psychophysics of Music, Heidelberg Science Library, Vol. 16,* English University Press Ltd.

Roederer, J. G. (1973). Psychophysics of Musical Perception, Colorado: Department of Physics, Denver University Research Institute

Ross, James E. (1958). *Groundwork of Educational Psychology,* G. Harrap

Sadler, J. E. and Gillett, A. N. (1965). *Training for Teaching,* Novello

Sandor, Frigyes (1969). *Musical Education in Hungary,* Budapest: Corvina

Sargant, W. (1957). *Battle for the Mind,* Pan Books

Schafer, R. Murray (1956). *The New Soundscape,* BMI, Canada, Ltd.

Schafer R. Murray (1965). *The Composer in the Classroom,* Ontario, Canada: Berandol Music Ltd.

Schafer, R. Murray (1967). *Ear Cleaning,* Ontario: Berandol Music Ltd.

Schafer, R. Murray (1970). *When Words Sing,* Ontario: Berandol Music Ltd.

Scholes, Percy. A. (1955). *The Oxford Companion to Music,* Oxford University Press

Schonell, F. (1952). *The Psychology and Teaching of Reading,* Oliver and Boyd

Schonell, F. (1962). *Backwardness in the Basic Subjects,*

Oliver and Boyd

Schonell, F. (1962). Simple Prose Reading Test, R2

Schools Council Project (1971). *Music Education of Young Children, Report on Questionnaire for College Lecturers and Music Advisers,* University of Reading

Schools Council Research and Development Project (1971). *Music Education of Young Children. First Report and Plans for the Future,* University of Reading

Schuter, Rosamund (1964). *An Investigation of Hereditary and Environmental Factors in Musical Ability,* PhD thesis, University of London

Schuter, Rosamund (1974). *The Relationship between Musical Abilities and Personality Characteristics in Young Children,* ISME Seminar

Scott, D. (1976). *Understanding EEG*

Sealey, and Gibbon, V. (1969), *Communication and Learning,* Oxford: Blackwell

Seashore, Carl E. and Seashore, Harold (1934). The place of phonophotography in the study of primitive music. *Stud. the Psychol. Mus.,* **Vol. 79,** 485–487, University of Iowa

Seashore, Carl E. (1938). *Psychology of Music,* McGraw-Hill, p. 408

Seashore, Carl E. (1967). *Psychology of Music,* Dover Publications

Segler, H. (1974). *Innovations in Music Teaching, A Research Project,* ISME Seminar

Self, George (1967). *New Sounds in Class,* Universal Edition

Self, George (1969). *Aural Adventure,* Novello

Sergeant, Desmond (1969). *Pitch Perception and Absolute Pitch: Some Aspects of Musical Development,* Phd thesis, Reading University

Sergeant, Desmond and Thatcher, Gillian (1973). *Intelligence, Social and Musical Abilities*

Sheridan, M. (1969). *Development Progress of Infants,* London: HMSO

Sherman, A. H. (1935). *A Study of the Pitch Preferences of Children,* MA thesis, University of Syracuse

Silsbury, Elizabeth (1974). *Governmental Assistance to*

Music Education Research in Australia, ISME Seminar

Skinner, B. F. (1961). *Teaching Machines,* Freeman and Company

Small Christopher. *Black Cat,* Universal Edition

Smith, Edgar, H. (1953). The value of notated examples in learning to recognize musical themes aurally, *J. Res. Music Educ.,* **1,** 97–104

Smith, Frank (1971). *Understanding Reading,* Holt, Rinehart and Winston

Smith, Franklyn O. (1914). The effect of training in pitch discrimination, *Psychol. Monogr.,* **Vol. 17,** No. 3, 67–103

Smith and Miller (1966). *The Genesis of Language,* MIT Press

Smout, C. (1962). *Anatomy and Physiology,* E. Arnold

Sperling, A. (1972). *Psychology Made Simple,* Allen and Company

Spooner, V. (1978). *Orthoptics and Remedial Reading.*

Stannard-Allen, W. (1967). *Living English Speech,* Longmans

Stanton, Hazel M. (1935). *Measurement of Musical Talent – The Eastmand Experiment, University of Iowa Stud. Psychol. Music,* **2,** 1–140

Steiner, R. (1955). *Everything as Visible Speech,* R. Steiner Press

Steiner, R. (1967). *A Lecture on Eurythmy,* R. Steiner Press

Stephens, S. D. G. (1975). *The Input from a Damaged Ear,* Southampton: Institute of Sound Vibration Research

Stevens, S. S. and Davies, H. (1963). *Hearing, Its Psychology and Physiology,* John Wiley and Sons

Stokes, Charles F. (1944). *An Experimental Study of Tachistoscopic Training in Reading Music,* Phd thesis, University of Cincinnati

Stones, E. (1968). *An Introduction to Educational Psychology,* Methuen

Stones, E. (1968). *Learning and Teaching,* J. Wiley and Sons

Storr, Anthony (1975). *Creativity in Music,* Psychology of Music

Stouffer, James L., Doherty, E. Thomas, Hollien, Harry (1975), Effect of training on human underwater sound-localization ability, *J. Acoust. Soc. Amer.*, **Vol. 57,** No. 5

Swanwick K. (1968). *Popular Music and the Teacher,* Pergamon Press

Swanwick K. (1973). Musical cognition and aesthetic response, *Psychol. Mus,* **1,** 2

Suzuki, Dr. S. *The Suzuki Violin School,* Boosey and Hawkes

Suzuki, Dr. S. *Nurtured by Love,* Bosworth and Company Limited

Szabo, Helga (1969). *Kodaly Concept of Music Education,* Boosey and Hawkes

Szamara, Osztalya. *Enek – Zene,* Budapest: Tankony-vukiado

Szonyi, E. (1973). *Kodaly's Principles in Practice,* Corvina Press

Takahagi, Yasuharu (1974). *Research of Music Education in Japan,* ISME Seminar

Tansley, A. E. (1970). *Listening to Sounds,* Leeds: E. J. Arnold

Tansley, A. E. (1970). *Sound Sense,* Leeds: E. J. Arnold

Taylor, J. G. *A New Approach to the Problem of Audition,* University of Cape Town

Teplov, B. M. (1966). *Psychologie des Aptitudes Musicales,* Presses Universtaires de France

Thackray, Rupert (1974). *Tests of Feeling for Tonality,* ISME Seminar

Tibble, J. W. (1966). *Study of Education,* Routledge and Kegan Paul

Tobias (1970). *Foundation of Modern Auditory Theory,* New York Acadèmic Press

Trousdek, Campbell. *Profile of the Polish Music Schools,* Canada

Tudor-Hart, Beatrix (1969). *An Experiment in Methodology Using a Phonetic Alphabet: Spelling Progress Bulletin.*

Tudor-Hart, Beatrix. *Hearing to Speak, to Read, to Write. Write.*

Tyler, Ralph (1971). *Basic Principles of Curriculum and Instruction,* University of Chicago Press

Ufer, Joachem (1969). *The Principles and Practice of Hormone Therapy,* Berlin: W. Gruyter

Van Bodegraven, Paul (1949). Music reading, *Mus. Educ. J.,* **35,** 71–72

Van Camp, K. (1975). On irregular acoustic reflex patterns, *Scand. Audiol.,* **4**

Van der Sandt, W. – *A Survey of the Acuity of Hearing in the Kalahari Bushmen.*

Van der Sandt, W., Glorig, Aram and Dickson R. (1969). A survey of the acuity of hearing in the Kalahari Bushmen, *Inter. Audiol.,* **Vol. 3,** 290–8

Van Nuys, Kelvin and Weaver, Homer E. (1943). Memory span and visual pauses in reading rhythms and melodies, *Psychol. Monogr.,* **Vol. 55,** No. 1, 33–50

Van Uden – *Sound Perception Methods,* Holland: St Michielgestel Institute for the Deaf

Valletina (1977). Perceptual problems in reading, *Harvard Educ. Rev.*

Vernon, M. D. (1962). *The Psychology of Perception,* London: Penguin Books

Vernon, P. E. (ed.) (1972). *Creativity,* Penguin

Waldman, Cockcroft, Ludi (1974). Filtered music – a hearing test for young children, *S. African Med. J.*

Walker, K. (1962). *Human Physiology,* Pelican

Walker, K. (1968). *Human Physiology,* Penguin

Walton, J. N. (1977). *Essentials of Neurology,* Pitman

Warburton, A. (1973). *A Graded Music Course for Schools,* Longman

Ward, D. (1972). *Sound Approaches for Slow Learners,* Bedford Square Press

Weale, R. A. – *Sight to Light,* Oliver and Boyd

Weaver, Homer E. (1931). *An Experimental Study of Music Reading,* PhD thesis, Stanford University

Weaver, Homer E. (1943). A survey of visual processes in reading differently constructed muscial selections, *Psychol. Monogr.,* **Vol. 55,** No. 1, 30

Westphal, E. O. J. (1971). *Vowel Systems and X-Ray Photography,* University of Cape Town

Wheeler, D. K. (1971). *Curriculum Processes,* University of London Press

Wheeler, Lester R. and Wheeler, Viola D. (1952). The relationship between music reading and language abilities, *J. Educ. Res.,* **45,** 439–450

Whetnell, Edith and Fry, D. B. (1964). *The Deaf Child,* Heinemann Medical Books Ltd.

Whipple, (1903). Studies in pitch discrimination, *Amer. J. Psychol.,* **14,** 289–309

Wing, (1970). *Tests of Musical Ability,* Cambridge University Press

Wing, Herbert D. (1941). A factorial study of musical tests, *Br. J. Psychol.,* **31,** 341–355

Wing, Herbert D. (1948). Test of musical ability and appreciation, *Brit. J. Psychol. Monogr. Supplement No. 27,* Cambridge University, 88

Wisbey, Audrey S. (1976). *Pitch Memory Acquisition and the Implications for Music Education.*

Wolf, Johannes *Handbuch der Notationskunde I and II.*

Wolner, M. and Pyle, W. K. (1933). An experiment in individual training of pitch-dificient children, *J. Ed. Psychol.,* **24,** 602–608

Wood, A. (1944). *The Physics of Music,* Methuen

Wooldridge, Dean E. (1963). *The Machinery of the Brain,* McGraw-Hill Book Co.

Wright, Denis (1963). *The Complete Bandsman,* Pergamon Press

Wright, Frank (1957). *Brass Today,* Besson and Company

Wright, P. – *Evidence of Alternative Strategies and Sentence Retention,* Medical Reserve Council

Wright, Patricia and Kahneman, Daniel (1971). Evidence for alternative strategies of sentence retention, *J. Exper. Psychol.,* **Vol. 23,** 197–213

Wright and Taylor (1970). *Introducing Psychology,* Penguin

Wyatt, M. (1965). *Paediatrics.*

Wyatt, Ruth F. (1945). Improvability of pitch discrimination, *Psychol. Monogr.,* **Vol. 58,** No. 2, 58

Wynn, V. T. (1973). Absolute pitch in humans – its variations and possible connections with other known rhythmic phenomena, In *Process in Neurobiology,* Pergamon Press

Zinkins, Gottlieb, Schapiro (1978). Developmental and psychoeducational sequelae of chronic otitis media, *Amer. J. Dis. Child.,* **Vol. 132**

Zusne, (1970). *Visual Perception of Form,* Academic Press Inc.

Reports

A Framework for Expansion (1972). DES, HMSO

Changing the Curriculum (ed. J. F. Kerr) (1968). University of London Press

Concept of Education (ed. Peters) (1966). Routledge and Kegan Paul

Disorders of Auditory Function (ed. W. Taylor) (1971). London: Academic Press

Educational Research (1967). National Foundation of Educational Research

Experimental Secondary Schools of Music (1972). Polish Ministry of Culture

Frequency Analysis and Periodicity Detection in Hearing (1970). (ed. Plomp and Smovnenburg), Sijthoff and Leiden

Handbook of Health Education (1968). DES, HMSO

ISME Handbook (1971). Schotts

ISME Handbook (1974). Schotts

ISME Handbook (1975). Schotts

Musical Ability Utilization Project (1963). Washington Board of Education

New Medical Use for Tuning Forks (1972). *Lancet*

New Oxford History of Music. Oxford University Press

Principles of the International Phonetic Association (1970). International Phonetic Association

Progress in Objective Audiometry (1975). J. of Laryng., Volume 86.

Psychology of Music Journal (1975). Society for Research in Psychology of Music and Music Education

Sound Growth (1973). Beaufort School, England

Teacher Education and Training (1972). DES, HMSO

The Effects of Auditory and Visual Background on Apparent

Duration (1956). American Journal of Psychology

The Hungarian Music Education System (1970). University of Budapest

The Relationship between Pitch Discrimination and Phonic Ability in Young ESN Children; Dartington College of Arts, Devonshire, England

The New Curriculum, Prepared by Schools Council. HMSO

Yamaha Music School, Parents Handbook. Yamaha Internation Corp.